TINA!

Also by Steven Ivory

PRINCE

TINA!

Steven Ivory

BANTAM BOOKS
TORONTO • NEW YORK • LONDON • SYDNEY • AUCKLAND

TINA

A Bantam Book/January 1986

ISBN 0-553-17199-2

Published simultaneously in the United States and Canada

Bantam Books are published by Bantam Books, Inc. Its trademark,
consisting of the words "Bantam Books" and the portrayal of a
rooster, is Registered in U.S. Patent and Trademark Office and in
other countries. Marca Registrada. Bantam Books, Inc., 666 Fifth
Avenue, New York, New York 10103.

Printed and bound in Great Britain by
Cox & Wyman Ltd., Reading

O   0 9 8 7 6 5 4 3 2 1

ACKNOWLEDGMENTS

I'd love to take total credit for this work, but there were many people who contributed to this project in many different ways: my agents, Bart Andrews and Sherry Robb, who represent me with strength, love and understanding. I heartfully thank the two of you for taking care of me. My editor, Adrienne Ingrum, and her assistant, Joe Pheifer. What can I say, Adrienne? I absolutely love experiencing the warmth and determination with which you perform your duties. You make it all so painless. I already know you're one of the best.

Michael Ochs and Lynne Richardson of the Michael Ochs Archives—thank you for opening your facilities to me. Music journalists everywhere owe it to themselves to visit and support this place (45 Breeze Ave., Venice, California 90291); they're looking out for our history! Thank you, Denise Hall, for once again getting me started on the manuscript; you could make a living doing that. Thanks to Carla Glover—appreciate your time and energy. Thanks to Mrs. Williams, Johnson Publishing Company, Chicago—you're a lifesaver. Appreciation to Michele Elyzabeth and all the other sources who shared with me their experiences of the Revue. Thanks to Bob Burchman. I've enjoyed your friendship. Thanks to the Fellas: Lee Bailey and *Radioscope*,

Nelson George and Miles White ("I think you're gonna need something stronger than No Doz this time . . .").

I appreciate your contribution: Sgt. John P. Plunkett; *Black Beat* magazine; John and Marjorie Ivory/Ivorys; Mary Minnis; Jessie, Christine and Jewel Turner; Miss Holmes, Miss Davis and everyone from 6th and High, Okla City; Pasta by Intermezzo on Melrose. I remember the couch, Gerald Wayne. Thank you for your love and patience, Anne McLaren. Hello to my friends in Glasgow, Scotland. Thank you, James T. McDonough, for sharing with me The Power.

*Dedicated with love and appreciation
to the memory of Clifford Minnis,
the prototype of a true gentleman.*

TINA:
Love (soul and determination) has got
everything to do with it. You are an inspiration to
anyone within
the sound of your voice.
Thank you.

Contents

PROLOGUE: Private Dancer,   13
     Public Comeback
1. Anna Mae Bullock   19
2. The Almighty Revue   34
3. Ike's Empire   48
4. Nowhere to Go but Up   80
5. A New Beginning   94
6. Tina Turner the Burner   105
7. The Making of a Superstar   135
8. The Queen Is Crowned   149
EPILOGUE: A Star Is Reborn   161
DISCOGRAPHY   179

Tina Turner is now the hottest female star on the pop music scene, but it wasn't easy. After surviving almost countless dues-paying performances and a tumultuous

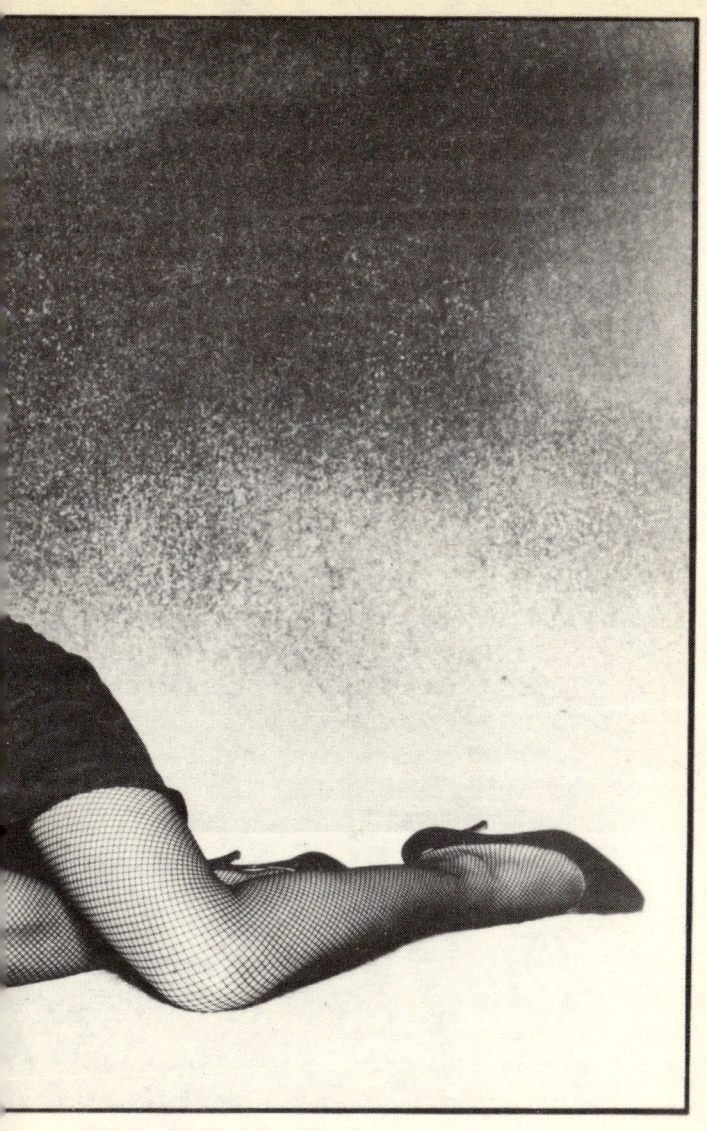

relationship with Ike Turner, she sings with an urgency that could only be heartfelt—one of the qualities that makes her so special. *Photo courtesy of Capitol Records.*

Prologue
Private Dancer, Public Comeback

"People all over the world keep asking me when I'm going to slow down, but I'm just getting started!"—Tina to a recent concert audience.

Wednesday morning, February 27, 1985. Gregory Peck is on the phone. Not his secretary, but the distinguished actor himself, known for his many stellar performances, including *Roman Holiday, Moby Dick, To Kill a Mockingbird* (for which he won an Oscar for Best Actor) and *The Omen*. It seems Peck happened to catch the Grammy Awards on television the night before, when he discovered the glory of Tina Turner. Turner officially tasted victory three times that night, and Peck, apparently enamoured with Turner's winning way, was moved to phone Tina for a date, so to speak. Reportedly, he was on the phone to Roger Davies, the man who manages the superstar's affairs, with a formal invite for Tina to accompany him to the Oscar ceremonies one month later. Peck's call was but one of many that same day from strangers who phoned about everything from offers of grandiose movie deals to contracts for product endorsements. Perhaps some of the others fared better than Peck: "Turner will be on tour in Europe the day of the Oscars," he was informed.

Everyone loves a winner, and on the night of the Grammys, Turner won big. *Private Dancer,* Turner's first recording in years, garnered awards for Best Rock Performance by a Female, Best Pop Performance by a Female and Best Record of the Year. However, Grammy night was only symbolic for Tina, who in 1985 won much more than Grammys. This year, the awards merely served as a grand salute to the fact that she had finally gained full control of her life.

It is hard to believe that the lady striding time and again to the glitter-laden stage that night was the same person who spent sixteen years suffering privately in a marriage that ultimately turned into a public nightmare; who poured her talents into building a legendary entertainment duo, only to lose everything but her sanity in the end; whose record company publicity department, only months before the Grammys presentation, had to lure reporters to the press conference promoting the release of *Private Dancer* with the firm announcement that yes, refreshments *would* be served; who, as late as the period during which "What's Love Got to Do with It" was at the top of the single charts, was playing out the last of the lounge-show convention commitments she'd relegated herself to for several years in order to pay off huge financial debts incurred in the past. What's even harder to believe is that this same woman was the architect and builder of one of the biggest, most sterling comebacks anyone in the history of pop music has ever enjoyed. By comparison, winning three peculiar-looking gold-plated paperweights seemed like child's play. For Tina Turner, 1985 was more than a musical victory. It marked a *human* triumph. The star-studded Grammy ceremony simply served as Ms. Turner's glorified coming-out party.

At the moment, Tina Turner is the most popular female in pop music. Grittier than Barbra Streisand and Diana Ross, and mature enough to teach Madonna and Cyndi

Lauper a thing or two about life, Turner is the embodiment of the rock and roll she so valiantly sings. With legs up to here and her sexy but womanly demeanor, Turner is, by far, pop music's most successful female rocker.

Turner's comeback, though rousing, should be of little surprise to anyone who closely examines the woman. Just like a hit record of the fifties can be rearranged, recorded and refined into an eighties smash, so is Tina's resilience. Probably more than any other female rocker, Turner personifies the term rock and roll. Her life has rocked with the good times and rolled with the punches. She is one of the few vocalists who can take a song and truly make it her own. How else could she and Ike, her former husband and mentor, as Ike and Tina Turner, build a veritable career on singing the songs of others? They took songs like John Fogerty's "Proud Mary," originally done by Fogerty's band Creedence Clearwater Revival, and molded them into true rock 'n' soul classics. It is the kind of ability that has made Tina a true queen of rock and roll among such rock royalty as the Rolling Stones, guitarist Jeff Beck and David Bowie, all of whom Tina counts among her favorite people.

"Tina is *real*," Keith Richards of the Stones has said. "When that woman opens her mouth, you feel that stuff. You're not thinking, Who wrote this song? or, Man, that arrangement is nice. You're thinking, Jeezus, this woman is singing her ass off. You're thinking, Man . . . I *feel* this. She reaches in for your heart. That's supposed to be what [rock and roll] is all about, isn't it?"

Aiding Turner's popularity more than any record company promotional campaign could is the singer's own persona. Even an executive at Capitol Records agreed that Tina Turner the Woman actually sold more records than any advertisement could. "One of the things we learned early is that, number one, Tina Turner was a name that everyone knew," he said. "Number two, we learned that *Private Dancer* could appeal to all kinds of people—to black people, to college kids, to blue-collar workers. As far as some of these buying groups are concerned, I believe Tina's reputation—her life and what she's gone through—had a lot to do with it. I'm not saying everyone who purchased the album knew her life story and could relate, but directly or indirectly, I believe that *is* the case. Either you know about those struggling years, or if you're some mountain man living in the woods, you simply relate to the emotion in the music."

That's a general analysis of Tina's new success. Specifically, her following can be broken down into other categories. There is, of course, her enormous talent as a singer and unique interpreter of a composer's lyrics. However, there is also a sexual component, the physical attraction of this provocative woman. More significant is the fact that to many women, Turner serves as a heroine and role model, a woman who has survived amidst chauvinism, sexism and other burdens that come with being a "woman in a man's world," according to Turner. "I'm very aware of that appeal I have to women. But I want to extend beyond just women; I suspect we all have some cross to bear. But it's easy for a woman to sometimes feel we're simply objects in a man's world."

1

Anna Mae Bullock

"It's a classic now, but when I wrote it I hated that track. It drove me crazy because that guitar was the only thing on it until I did the vocal. Really and truly, I just wrote how we lived. I should do some more like that."—Tina talking about the song "Nutbush City Limits."

Nutbush, Tennessee, sounds like a small place. It is. Even today, Nutbush, like the colony of other little dirt-road towns in the South, can seem as if it isn't connected with the rest of the world. The COLORED ONLY signs have long since disappeared from the outside of eating places, restrooms and small establishments that make up this little town, but people still know where and where not to go. In many ways, Nutbush, just fifty miles from Memphis, is a godforsaken town. Perhaps because of that, Nutbush will go down in history as the place where Tina Turner was born on November 26, 1939, ten years after the start of America's economically crippling depression. When outsiders go to Nutbush inquiring about Tina, the locals correct you with a certain amount of pride. Tina's real name, they are quick to point out, is Anna Mae Bullock. Anna Mae was the second of two children—both daughters—born to Floyd and Zelma Bullock.

Floyd, a stoutly religious man (Baptist, of course), worked as a sharecropper managing farm territory, aided by his wife of half–Cherokee Indian descent, which accounts for Tina's high cheekbones and, according to Indian legend, her forever lithe, youthful figure.

The idea of picking cotton and fruit, which is what the family did to support themselves, may sound like a meager way to make a living, especially in the forties, when America was just a decade away from the golden modern fifties, but actually this was good work in the South if you could get it. Most importantly, it was steady. When tended to, the land never stopped giving, and when you're working around food, you'll almost always have some of it to feed your family. At that time in a town where white folks were often as bad off as the blacks, the Bullock family lived fairly well. Their dwelling, though small, accommodated the family well, and outside they had a bit of a farm with pigs and chickens scattered about. That's still good living by Southern small-town standards, even today.

Anna's musical education came the way most black musicians got theirs, via the Baptist Church. Anna used to wail in the choir on Sundays, and during the week, she'd work out with whatever came on the radio, mainly hard-core country music but some blues as well, including Muddy Waters, Howlin' Wolf, Bobby "Blue" Bland and B. B. King, who even then was considered name-brand blues.

"I used to always sing," Tina said years later. "Out in the fields picking cotton, around the house—I was always singing. I used to really get involved in the church thing—the dancing and carrying on. I didn't really understand what it was all about, but the music and the feeling moved me. It's the same way onstage, even today. The music starts and I have to move."

Eventually, circumstances in Anna's family forced her to move. Her parents separated while she was still in her teens, and her mother Zelma migrated to St. Louis while her father worked his way to Chicago. Anna and her older sister, Eileen, went with their mother, and Anna enrolled in a St. Louis school. Eileen took a job in a local hospital, and Anna later did the same. Soon both were plugged into St. Louis night life, which was a big deal to two girls who grew up entertaining themselves by singing. Eileen used to hit a couple of places, some of them little holes in the wall powered by jukeboxes stocked with plenty of R & B platters. One of her favorite stops was a funky little spot in East St. Louis called the Club Manhattan.

Club Manhattan in the mid fifties was as close as a St. Louis girl could get to the night life of New York. The men were handsome and dressed finely, and the women were mildly sophisticated. And of all the night spots, Manhattan offered the best live music. Anna used to beg Eileen to take her into the place, but big sister always said something to the effect that Anna was only sixteen, which *really* meant big sis didn't want the dead weight. But when Anna turned seventeen, Eileen *did* let Anna come along, and Tina still recalls the feeling of stepping through the doors of the place for the first time. "It was . . . electric; there all of these people were, smoking cigarettes and drinking. It was such a hip place to be. I felt like I crossed some kind of barrier. I felt like a lady, all grown up."

Undoubtedly, one of the causes of Anna's euphoric headiness was the same reason the club was so popular: the bandstand. Club Manhattan offered some of the best live music around, and one of the crowd's favorites was a group called the Kings of Rhythm, headed by a cool, stone-faced organist and guitar player by the name of Ike Turner.

Ike was born Izear Luster Turner in Clarksdale, Mississippi, in 1931 on the fifth of November—the same month as Anna. Ike, a preacher's son, has said his career first started when he used to play an old piano "in a church lady's house. She would let me play her piano in exchange for chopping wood for her. I learned to play some popular tunes on that piano, but pretty soon I wanted my own. So I started nagging my mother for a piano, and she told me if I got good grades, she'd think about it. When school was out that year, I came home with a report card full of A's and B's. I walked in the house and there it was, a new piano, and she said it was all mine. It was like a dream come true, and that was the real beginning of my career."

And that is generally how Ike Turner looked at music from the very beginning—as a career. He was always looking to jam with other kids who were musicians, and while some of them could "hang," many of them were put off by Turner's drive to turn things into a professional situation. His father wasn't thrilled with his son's zeal for secular music but reluctantly looked the other way when Ike formed the original Kings of Rhythm unit while he was still in high school.

In 1951, when the band huddled in producer Sam Phillips' famed Sun Studio in Memphis and cut a ragged little jump tune called "Rocket 88," the single's credits were supposed to read "Ike Turner Band featuring Jackie Brenston," but somehow ended up as "Jackie Brenston and his Delta Cats." Regardless, the track has since been unofficially heralded as the first rock and roll record. In 1951, however, the honor was worth little more than a few bucks and a little notoriety, which wore off quickly.

In 1956 Ike and the Kings moved into East St. Louis, where they set up headquarters in a big house. His band had to live with him, not only for expense purposes, but also so that Ike could run the band through rehearsal at 10 A.M. if he wanted to. "Ike was brutal to work for," reflected St. Louis recording entrepreneur Bill Stevens. "It took stamina to work with him. Ike once kicked a man offstage at the Club Imperial for missing a note. But that's how he got things done. He was a hustler."

The big house where the band lived also served as home for Ike's common-law wife and the two sons they had together. Women. That was Ike's other passion. Not considered a Romeo by general standards, Ike never had any problem with women. They all seemed to be attracted to his cool—he could definitely be considered the silent type—but strong-willed ways. Most of the women Ike saw intimately were impressed first by his willingness to provide and then by the determined fervor with which he pursued his career in music. That attraction was ironic since, after he became comfortable with the relationship, it would usually take a backseat to Ike's musical pursuits.

Once the band was settled in, Ike immediately began dropping in on local club owners, lining up gigs. Soon he had worked out a system whereby the band could make some decent money, but they had to play at least three clubs a night. For instance, by the time the band would work the Club Manhattan, they had normally already played full sets at two other clubs, and if they could squeeze it in, a private white house-party on the other side of town.

It was appropriate, however, that Club Manhattan always be the last stop on the Kings' nightly local tour, since the band would have warmed their chops enough to dispense with the Top 40 stuff they played at the white clubs and parties and lean into heavy-duty R & B and smoky-room blues. Ike would direct the band through a driving repertoire of tunes made popular by black artists such as Ray Charles, Little Willie John and Muddy Waters, mixed in with originals. This would go on until the wee hours of the morning.

Regardless of his modest beginnings Ike went on to have an expensive, if not illustrious, career in the music industry, and in terms of the time he's spent in the business, Ike's career makes Tina's seem minute. Before he and Anna met, Ike had worked and recorded for a legion of labels, including Vita, Federal, Tunetown, Cobra/Artistic and Chess. He'd later earn some local notoriety with his recording of "Hey Hey" on the Stevens label, under the name of Icky Renrut— Turner spelled backwards. It seems Turner didn't want to wait out a contract with another company and used the name to go undetected. He also recorded under the banner of the Tophatters, another band he headed.

Anna Mae had become a semiregular at the Club Manhattan during Ike's stint there by the time she conjured up the nerve to approach him about singing with the band one night. Every now and then someone would go onstage and sing a song with the Kings, and Anna figured she was as good as—even better than—some of the men and women who would get up there and growl. But unless Ike heard a woman's voice first, usually the only thing that made him look twice at a female was her curves, and at seventeen, Anna Mae was the scrawny little thing Ike kept promising a chance, only to turn to another woman from the bevy that sought him out night after night at the club. But Anna was insistent, and when she was suddenly faced with the chance to be heard, she took it.

"One night," she told an interviewer years later, "when the drummer put a microphone in front of my sister for her to sing, she refused and I took the mike and just started singing. Some B. B. King tune, I believe. I just let loose, and everybody came running in to see who it was." Anna ended up doing a whole impromptu set of songs with the band that night, and after the smoke cleared, Ike, rather embarrassed, admitted that he'd been wrong about not giving her a chance to pit her pipes with the Kings. "I didn't know you could *really* sing," he offered.

Not long after, Ike offered Anna a position singing with the band. In the beginning, she'd show up at the Club Manhattan and she'd wing it with the group, but soon, she'd become a bona fide member of the troupe, with Ike springing for stage clothes—fancy stuff like long gloves and pumps—that made her look older. For Anna, this was the pot of gold at the end of the rainbow. "I wasn't really making any money or anything," she recalls, "but still, just to be able to do something like that—wearing these clothes and standing up there singing with this band—I thought I had died and gone to heaven."

This was the beginning of Anna's career as an entertainer. During this period, she and Ike were more like big brother and little sister, with Ike taking more of a fatherly interest in her personal life than anything else. In fact, about this time, Anna was involved with another member of the Kings band. In 1958, after her graduation from high school, she became the mother of the musician's son. "It was bad enough that I was pregnant," she remembers. "I had to finish school or my mother would have gone crazy." Anna liked the idea of motherhood; when you were from a place like Nutbush, one of the best things you could do was settle down with a good man and have kids. However, Anna had stumbled upon this thing called entertaining—she says she never really went into it with thoughts of building a career—and thus, Raymond Craig, as her son was named, spent a lot of time with babysitters.

The Club Manhattan was fine, but Ike had his sights set on bigger things. Recording "Rocket 88" had left him with the yearning to make it as a nationally known recording artist. He'd always be able to arrange dates for the band, but with hit records the work would come to him, and lining up shows would be a lot easier. Soon, at rehearsals and between setup time on the stage, Ike was talking incessantly about the idea of journeying to California—Hollywood—to do some recording and try to get a recording contract. As Ike focused more on the professional aspect of his life, he paid less attention to the personal part, namely, his common-law wife. Suddenly Ike was paying more attention to scrawny Anna, and his concern for her went beyond whether she was singing out of key or what she wore onstage. Suddenly Ike had an intimate interest in his young protégée. For Anna, the sensation was strange and unwanted; she liked Ike as a friend; he'd virtually become her father. But increasingly Ike made his desires clear. He wanted to travel to L.A. and he wanted Anna to come with him.

While Ike was breaking up with his common-law wife, he was busy putting together another recording session. He had penned a song, "A Fool in Love," for a member of the Kings of Rhythm to sing, but Art Lassiter, that singer, was one of the few guys in the band who was as hardheaded as Ike was determined to maintain control. Ike and Lassiter argued often—about money, about music, about the direction of the Kings. And while their verbal bouts weren't unusual, this time Lassiter had one up on Ike, because Ike needed him to sing on the "Love" demo. On the day of the session, Lassiter was nowhere to be found.

Ike wasn't about to attempt singing the song himself. He considered others in the band, and Anna immediately came to mind. After all, she was familiar with the song— she'd heard it plenty of times while Ike was composing it—and the tight situation turned itself into an opportunity. "He just asked me to sing the song," Tina recalled. "I had no idea what he wanted to do with it. At most, I figured he just needed a voice on the track to peddle the record."

In being stood up by Lassiter, Ike learned a lesson that he'd incorporate into his business routine. Legend has it that Ike and Tina Turner records were released on so many different labels (see Discography) because, when Ike would have disagreements with a particular label, he'd pull out old tracks he had recorded earlier, and lease them to other labels, just to show companies he could not be stifled. The lesson learned was always to have a backup plan. In this case, Tina was the backup. (About this time, Ike recorded Anna singing another song as well, called "Letter to Tina," and offered it to entrepreneur Bill Stevens who turned it down, saying Tina "screamed" too much on the track.)

In any case, a man named Juggy Murray, who ran Sue Records in New York, liked "A Fool in Love," and gave Ike a recording contract. The record became a runaway national hit in 1960. While the record was working its way up the charts, Ike was busy putting together an act. In his head, he already knew what he wanted. As a kid, he fell in love with a Tarzan-like jungle queen movie character who wore skimpy, revealing animal rags and long hair down her back. "I used to be in love with that girl in that movie," Ike once told a television reporter. "That's where I got the idea for how Tina would look onstage."

Today, Tina agrees: "The basic sound, our look—that was totally Ike's concept. He came up with the idea of wigs and the short dresses. That was his image of sexiness. That's what he wanted me to look like."

However, Anna didn't learn much about Ike's plan until it was already in motion. In fact, Tina has said that she didn't learn about Ike's decision to give her a new name until she read the credits on the 45. "A Fool in Love" by Ike and Tina Turner. Whether she liked it or not, she was stuck with it. Some members of the band still called her Anna in the beginning, but Ike slowly prodded them into using the new handle. He himself had no problems adapting. Slowly, he was molding Anna into his idea of what a woman should be.

"A Fool in Love" was the record Ike had been praying for. The disc had "legs," a term used in the music industry to mean that a record had staying power. Ike prepared the band to go on the road. He rounded up three female background singers, dubbed them the Ikettes, and then Tina got sick. "I came down with jaundice," Tina remembered. "I was yellow all over, and I had to be hospitalized. I stayed there for about a month, when Ike came in one day and insisted that I was well enough to tour." So Tina left the hospital—without the blessings of her doctor—and hit the road. The Ike and Tina Turner Revue was born.

2

The Almighty Revue

"They'll be short; that way they're easy to pack."—Tina on the costumes she plans to wear on her 1985 concert tour.

Today it is truly a small wonder that Tina Turner doesn't see a car, bus, plane—*anything* that suggests travel—and run the other way in spasms. The woman has spent virtually a lifetime traveling across the planet, visiting places that, excepting their nightclubs and arenas, she has never really seen. Nevertheless, according to Tina, it is the only life she's really ever known. "That is an entertainer's life; that's part of it," she has said. "Sometimes I'd like to think I could just walk away from it all and just be a housewife, but at this point, I think I'd be bored stiff."

This insatiable wanderlust began in 1961, when the Ike and Tina Turner Revue hit the backroads of America, covering land Charles Kuralt never knew existed. Life on the road ain't easy for anyone, but for a woman, it can really be rough. Especially the fashion in which the Revue toured. "It was a great experience," said a former vocalist who was one of the many Ikette background singers employed at one time or another by Ike. She agreed to discuss the early Ike and Tina days, though she insisted on anonymity. ("Those days are over for me.") "When I say great, I don't necessarily mean great as in good, though it was a good experience for someone like me who, at the time, thought I really wanted to be in show business. I mean great, as in overwhelming. We were like a traveling circus. Maybe family is a better term. For me, it was mostly positive, but it wasn't always fun. Sometimes we'd have to sleep in the car or on the bus. Unless we pulled into a town where somebody knew somebody, home cooking was out of the question."

According to the ex-Ikette, playing the live performances wasn't so bad. The tough part was having to lend your talents to the late-night sessions that went on in almost every town *after* you did your two shows a night. "Every town we went to, Ike would get situated and then start looking for a recording studio to record in. He and the band had these tunes . . . Ike was always looking for the next hit tune."

The retired singer said that things on the road could have been worse had Ike not had a devout, if not fatherly, dedication to his band. "Especially the girls. He'd always ask me, 'You hungry? Have y'all eaten yet?' On the one hand, the sense of security was great, but then come that night onstage and you realized he wanted you to eat and get plenty of rest because he didn't want you messin' up when the show started. He was hell to deal with when it came to that."

Today, the ex-Ikette has left the music scene altogether, insisting "the only music I hear is what my kids bring home. But I do listen to Tina. I think it's amazing that she lasted through all we went through and *still* had enough left for a second career. But that's what happens when it gets in your blood. It's like running away and joining the circus or the army. If it gets in your system, you can't get it out. I have to salute her."

Considering the circumstances, it didn't take long for the girls Ike had enlisted from

St. Louis to drop out, one by one. Disgruntled, Ike would simply hire new girls in each town. Nevertheless, if the working conditions had been all Tina had had to deal with, things would have been fine, but there was also the fact that, according to the ex-Ikette, Ike suddenly decided that he wanted to go back to the mother of his two sons. "I know it must have upset Tina. . . . I mean, I think she was embarrassed by his actions more than anything. I say that because Ike wasn't too discreet with anything. If he wanted to curse one of the musicians, he did it right then and there. But I say she was more embarrassed than hurt, because—and this is just my personal opinion—I think Tina wanted to get out of the whole thing. Let's face it, she was young; if not young agewise, definitely young to the world. And I think at some point she must have known she didn't want to spend the rest of her life with Ike. She had to know it. Maybe she just didn't trust her feelings. I myself witnessed at least three times that she should have gone back to her mother in St. Louis."

To further complicate this emotional twist of events, Tina discovered that she was pregnant by several weeks with Ike's child. Once Ike discovered this, he promptly had a change of heart and continued with Tina, insisting that they get married. "I remember Ike saying, 'Yeah, I think I'm gonna go ahead and make this thing legal,'" said the ex-Ikette. "At that point, I didn't know whether to be happy or sad for Tina." The singer says that even though she feels Tina wasn't too crazy about the idea, "she got all excited about the fact that she was getting hitched—until she found out where they were going to do it."

Tijuana, Mexico, is where Ike took Tina to tie the knot. "The next time I saw Tina, she seemed pretty miserable," said the singer. "She was thinking of a gown and flowers, and I understand they just signed a piece of paper and that was it."

With that out of the way, Ike and Tina went back to making records and touring. The single, "I Idolize You," was the follow up to "A Fool in Love." Musically, Ike was progressing in the sense that he'd finally hit the pulse of a wider audience. The songs he wrote and accepted from the band increasingly avoided the gutbucket blues flavor he'd been raised on as he became more aware of—and frustrated with—the racism he found prevalent in the music business. No matter how mainstream his music sounded (at least in his opinion), the more difficult it became to create a record that reached into the white pop charts the way "Fool in Love" did.

In retrospect, the ex-Ikette now sees a connection between Ike and Tina's song titles and Ike and Tina's relationship. "It probably means nothing, but I think back on it now and it's kind of strange. I mean, 'A Fool in Love'? That's what we used to playfully call Tina behind her back. 'I Idolize You'? *C'mon.* Sounds like something Ike wanted to hear." In fact, Ike's ex-employee says that she believes that right after the marriage, Tina began slowly to realize that she had been corralled by what the Ikette referred to as "that man-woman thing." "That's when a man is there for a woman and he makes everything so right. Either the woman is too young to have experienced anything like it, or she's old enough to have had her share of rotten apples. She may not exactly be in love with the man, but he's better than what she's been dealing with before. And things are too secure to go out there looking for something else. That's what Tina was caught up in for most of her life with Ike."

Even Tina, in looking back, has confided that "perhaps I knew I didn't want the relationship, but it was all I had then." There was also a certain element of fear of leaving. That fear came from physical abuse Ike inflicted, a ritual Tina says began shortly after the contract signing with Sue Records in 1960. And according to that former background vocalist, Tina wasn't the only one who received physical abuse when Ike's emotions lost out to his frustrations. "I saw him knock one of the girls [Ikettes] around once. The problem was that Ike, in many ways, was a perfectionist. He wasn't a *bad* man—let me make that clear—but he had a lot of things pent up inside of him, things that were there long before the Ike and Tina thing. It was a human emotional problem, not created by show business, but aggravated by it, for sure."

Whatever Ike's problem was, when he didn't succumb to it, things were fine. Tina has, in fact, remarked in interviews that she "had some good times with Ike; I remember his sense of humor. When he cared, things were good." Musically, Ike's determination seemed boundless. By 1960, the band had developed into a supertight performing unit, and when the troupe hit the stage, it was like being taken by a musical tidal wave. As for Tina, you had to compare her to male entertainers; there weren't very many women who could keep pace with her up there. Every night, in one supper club or another, she'd come strutting out into the spotlight, shimmy up to the microphone and proceed to guide the Ikettes and her audience through a series of cut-the-rag antics. The Ike and Tina Turner Revue moved like a machine. None of it ever seemed spontaneous; it was meant to look rehearsed. Ike used to say, "When people pay to see you, they come to be *entertained,* not to see mistakes. They can do that at home in the mirror." The Revue was an action-packed potpourri of bold soul moves, driving R & B and some predetermined humorous banter between Tina and Ike. All in all, the presentation was a hybrid of sexy burlesque and Vegas gaudiness. To the untrained eyes of much of the audience, Tina looked like the only star of the show. That was the way Ike planned it. However, in the background, usually just behind the Ikettes and often wearing dark shades, was Ike, strumming some scratchy rhythm guitar, pumping the band and working as the show's catalyst. Tina, years after the breakup, said, "I never felt that he got enough credit for what went on up there. He got some incredible sounds out of his guitar. He never received his propers as a musician."

However, as hard as Tina shimmied onstage, her job offstage was formidable, as Ike generally saw her role away from the spotlight as that of his servant. She served his meals, manicured his hands and feet, did his hair and then got out of his way to let him pursue music activities.

And the hits kept coming. Some of the Ike and Tina efforts that made the black music charts had titles like "It's Gonna Work Out Fine," "Poor Fool," "Tra La La La La" and "You Should'a Treated Me Right." These weren't records that exactly captivated the nation, but they certainly had enough potency to keep the Revue in demand on the "chitlin' circuit," that almighty territory of small black supper clubs, smoky rooms and soul lounges that served as an umbilical cord for black acts on the way up or on the way down in their careers.

The action kept Ike and Tina on the road so much that when they finally did move into a Los Angeles home about 1965, it still took Tina almost a year to actually get to know the town. Touring for most of the year meant the money was getting better, and so were the physical surroundings. But emotionally things were deteriorating rapidly. Tina was growing more dissatisfied with her occupation as Ike's pet. Her woes, however, were always overshadowed by yet another development in her career, one that had all the makings of a grand opportunity for the duo.

In 1965, the Ike and Tina Turner Revue was wearing out the stage of Cyrano's, then a hot nightspot located on Hollywood's Sunset Boulevard. Unbeknownst to the band, Phil Spector, the record producer renowned for his big success with sixties pop soul and the guiding light for his girl group, the Ronettes, was in the audience. After watching Tina and company kill this audience, Spector had two thoughts. One, the group's electrifying performance would be great for a concert film he had a part in, called *The Big TNT Show*. But his first and foremost interest in Ike and Tina Turner was its fiery, big-voiced lead singer. He wanted to produce her. While he was familiar with Ike and Tina's work on wax, he felt he had a song that would be perfect for Tina, a tune he cowrote with two other writers entitled, "River Deep–Mountain High." Spector had many other musical vehicles for the tune, particularly the Ronettes, but he felt it needed a special kind of gutsy lead vocal. A vocal he immediately heard Tina supplying.

After the show, while Tina and the rest of

the musicians tended to themselves backstage, Spector introduced himself to Ike and
told him his ideas right on the spot. There
was one thing Spector said that made Ike
hedge at first. Spector wanted to produce
Tina, but only Tina. He wasn't interested in
having Ike or his band involved. It was nothing personal; Spector had his own musicians
who had helped him establish his trademark
"wall of sound," and he didn't want to tam-
per with a formula. Besides, Spector had already recorded the instrumental track. In his
opinion, the only thing between the track
and the number one position on the national
music charts was Tina's glory singing on it.

Ike pondered the situation for a couple of
days. He was well aware of Spector's hit status and reputation; he viewed the association
as just the opening in the pop market he had
been looking for. Ike had a meeting with
Spector. He was interested in working with
him, but he had only one stipulation: that the
record, even though it didn't include him
and the band, still be credited to Ike and
Tina Turner. Spector had no objections to
that; the deal was on.

The day of the session, Ike took Tina over
to the Gold Star studio in Hollywood, not far
from the club where Spector and Ike had

met. Ike was fairly optimistic that day, but didn't let Tina begin the project without grumbling something about not messing things up. Ike saw this session as the duo's key to the Big Time—he didn't want Tina (the only reason Spector was interested in the Revue) to mess things up.

Spector had met Tina briefly that night at Cyrano's, but it wasn't until the session that she was one-on-one with him, and she was immediately comfortable. Today, Tina says she remembers him to be a very patient producer, very pleasant. For the first time, she really felt part of a situation. Despite the fact that she sang lead on all the Ike and Tina records and was the only one who officially fronted the band onstage, she was made to feel that her talents weren't indispensable. Spector made it clear how much he admired her ability. Also, for Tina there was the joy that "River Deep–Mountain High" was just a bit more melodic than what she'd been wailing with Ike. She'd later recount that in her opinion, "the material was more like rock and roll, and I've always liked rock and roll. It was exciting to have that opportunity and work with Phil at the same time."

However, like Ike—perhaps even more so—Spector was a perfectionist. With the recording engineer, Tina and that exhilarating music track, he went to work crafting Tina's vocal delivery. "That was tough," said Tina, "because everything went well except for the first line in the song. He had me do that one little sentence over and over until I got it right. . . . Well, let's just say, good enough that he just finally left it like that. It was a challenge to have that much asked of you. I was standing at the microphone drenched in perspiration."

Unfortunately, for all her sweat, when "River Deep–Mountain High" was released in 1966, it wasn't the success Spector, Ike and Tina had hoped for. While things were changing in America, they weren't changing fast enough for what Ike deemed to be that same old problem: racism. He told a reporter from *Soul* magazine, "If you're a black act, you have to prove yourself every time you make a record—no matter if your last record *did* crack the white market. 'River Deep' had what I thought were all the right ingredients. It was a pop record, white producer. But when it came time to get airplay, the black radio stations said it sounded too white; white stations said it was too black. It was an orphan record."

But that was the situation only in the

States. In England, the record became a big hit, climbing into the country's Top 5 on the charts. When "River Deep" became a hit in Europe, the Rolling Stones invited the group to open their 1966 European concert tour. Thus what was initially thought to be a failure turned out to be a blessing. Ike and Tina Turner were, after five years on the "chitlin' circuit," finally on their way to cracking the coveted pop music market.

3

Ike's Empire

*"Really? I wonder why?"—Tina's response
to a journalist's observation that she is
considered a sex symbol.*

The sixties turned out to be a banner decade
for Ike and Tina Turner; 1966 was the year
that the Revue garnered a streak of accomplishments that would free them from the
"chitlin' circuit" once and for all. That brief
European tour with the Stones was the beginning of it all. Ike and Tina were thrilled to
open dates for the rock band, and the Stones
were equally proud that Ike and Tina accepted the invitation. The Stones have been
called pop music's "most popular mock R &
B band." Mick Jagger has cited the Temptations, Smokey Robinson and the Ohio Play-

ers, not to mention a handful of obscure black blues artists, as their chief musical inspiration. To have bold-soulers like Ike and Tina opening their shows was considered an honor.

At the center of the group's attraction to the Revue was, of course, Tina. "She was just a terror," said Jagger about her performances to a music magazine reporter. "She would just come out there and give the crowd a workout. I used to hear her from backstage, *killin' 'em* and wonder if we did the right thing by fixin' it so we had to come *after* them. If she was white, she'd have been a superstar a long time ago."

It was during this period that Tina, Jagger and Stones guitarist Keith Richards would establish their mutual admiration society. "It was a great feeling to be playing for all these white kids," Tina remembers. "Back then, the feeling was that we were breaking the chains that were holding us back from a mass audience." In an interview with *Soul* magazine, Ike agreed. "When we played with the Stones, it told all the music industry people, the radio programmers, that 'Hey, this is a band that can reach *all* kinds of people. It took opening for the Rolling Stones for us to even *begin* to get that kind of respect."

According to Michele Elyzabeth, who was working as a music journalist in Paris when the Ike and Tina Turner Revue came to Europe for the first time in 1966, "It was an exciting period for everyone. I mean, Ike and Tina were *huge* in Europe. Huge. 'River Deep–Mountain High' may not have done anything in the States, but it made Tina a superstar in Europe. When 'Proud Mary' came out in Europe, it was like 'What's Love Got to Do with It' today. It was number one across the continent. Tina has always been big there."

So Elyzabeth was ecstatic when the European office of United Artists, Ike and Tina's label at the time, invited her to work as the group's host during the first leg of their tour. If that responsibility wasn't exciting enough, after Ike and Tina performed at a music convention in Paris, Tina asked Elyzabeth, a young French girl of twenty, if she would join the group for the remainder of their European tour, working as Tina's personal assistant. "I figured it was the chance of a lifetime, so I jumped at it. I was a big fan of their music."

According to Elyzabeth, the group went to London, where the night's performance had been sold out for days. The party situated itself at the London Hilton, and for the first time, Elyzabeth experienced Ike's other side. "We were there in Tina's suite—myself, some of the Ikettes, Ike and some other people. I don't know what the problem was, but suddenly, Ike just started hitting Tina—backhanding her, using his fists. Hitting her the way he'd hit a man. Tina never tried to fight back, and he was going crazy. In front of all these people. And this was forty-five minutes before the concert! That's one thing I came to understand about Ike. He didn't care *who* was in the room or listening or whatever. He'd hit her or call her some words that, at that age, I had to look up in the dictionary to learn what they meant.

"Anyway, that scared me to death. I don't know why I said it. They didn't know me; I'd just started working with them. But I told him that if he didn't stop right then, I'd call the police. No one else said anything. Then he stopped. I was stunned. Tina just got ready and went out on the stage, all black and blue and bleeding. Ike explained something about losing his head, but I noticed that no one seemed surprised but me. Another day we were riding in the limousine, and Ike said to me, 'You don't like me, do you?' I said, 'No, I don't.'"

For the next three months of the tour, Elyzabeth would serve as Tina's virtual shadow, taking her phone calls, taking care of all kinds of odds and ends. "My job was simple," she said. "Ike wanted me to tend to Tina—totally. That way, with somebody watching her, he could do whatever he wanted. That way, she was just out of his hair. But she never bothered him anyway." Between performances, when Tina and Elyzabeth were allowed mobility, they whiled away the hours in the streets of Europe, shopping. "Tina *loved* to shop," said Elyzabeth. "We would do that for hours. And there was never a shortage of money. She'd have her own money, but Ike would give me money as well, if he wanted something done. Tina always had a personal limousine twenty-four hours a day, which wasn't cheap in England. Tina's stage clothes were made by Azzaro, a major Italian designer. We stayed in five-star hotels. There was no expense spared."

Elyzabeth remembered that throughout her assignment with Tina the singer always seemed afraid. "She always seemed afraid of buying something, saying something, doing *anything* that would upset Ike. Never once while I was around her did she ever say anything bad about Ike or her condition. Not once. I noticed that she had old scars on her back and arms, and I got the nerve to ask her if Ike always treated her the way he did that night in London. That was her chance to complain, but she just mumbled something about him having a difficult temper."

Elyzabeth did get a glimpse of the motivating factor that held Tina's life together. "We'd eat dinner—just she and I—in her suite every night while Ike went partying. She'd never touch her food until she said a blessing over it. One day she said God would see her through and that everything would one day be all right. She seemed to be very religious, and I knew then that that's what kept her sane."

At one point, near the end of her work with the Revue, Tina, under instructions from Ike, offered Elyzabeth a permanent position with the entourage and asked that she join them in the States. "*That* was really something. In spite of everything, I got on very well with Tina and Ike; the opportunity to come to the States and work for them interested me, definitely. They told me I'd be working in Hollywood—I'd heard so much about the place." Enthusiastically, Elyzabeth accepted the offer.

Elyzabeth said she should have known
something was amiss when the plane ticket
that was promised her never reached Paris.
Nevertheless, determined to arrive on time
for her new job, Elyzabeth bought her own
ticket, gave notice at her job in Paris and
looked forward to her journey into Los Angeles. Once she was in L.A., there was no one
from the Revue's contingent to pick her up,
so "I just followed the Air France crew over
to the hotel they were staying in, near the
beach. I figured I would at least be safe staying where they stayed. I'd never been to Los
Angeles, and I didn't know a soul."

When she got to the hotel, Elyzabeth called
the Turner's residence. An aide answered
the phone, and what she told Elyzabeth
shocked her. "She said she was under orders
to tell me that I was fired," Elyzabeth said. "I
couldn't believe it. Here I was, in the middle
of a city—a *country*—I didn't even know, un-
able to speak English very well and being told
I was fired from a job I didn't even get a
chance to work at. The lady on the phone
said that Tina was not allowed to talk with me
and that I should not try to communicate
with Tina in any way. Then she hung up."

Elyzabeth said she spent the rest of the
week barraging the Turner home with calls.

"I was determined to reach Tina one way or another. I called constantly." Finally, she was given an appointment to see Tina at home. On the day of the meeting, she knocked on the door and was greeted by Ike's secretary. The secretary led Elyzabeth through the spacious home, where she found Tina in the kitchen. "She was in there without her wig, in everyday clothes, and she looked like she was cooking, sewing and doing something else, all at the same time. At that moment, she was possibly the most unhappy woman I had ever seen in my life." Tina smiled, wiped her hands and took Elyzabeth into another room. "She spoke real softly and told me this would be the first and last time she'd get a chance to speak with me. She said Ike was in the next room—when I first came in the house, he said hello and kept going—and that he would consider me a troublemaker if I kept being so persistent about the situation. The job was gone; she made that clear. But she was very nice. She offered me money, but I explained to her that I didn't come to the United States for a couple of bucks, I came to work."

Elyzabeth said she communicated with Tina once more over the phone, but that Tina pleaded in a whisper for her not to call again. "If Ike finds out I'm talking to you, he will be very upset," she told Elyzabeth. In retrospect, Elyzabeth, who now runs her own public relations and artist management company in Los Angeles, said she now realizes why Tina was stuck in her situation. "She was scared to death, constantly. Where would she go? Ike had all the *real* money and property. Looking back, I see how the Tina Turner the public sees—the sexy lioness—is just an image. In private, she didn't even *fit* the sexy image. In that kitchen that day, I saw the *real* Tina at the time—just another battered wife. I now also know that I didn't get the job because I told Ike how I felt about him that day in the limousine."

Elyzabeth ran into Tina Turner again at a party for a Grammy Awards presentation several years before the performer's 1985 comeback. "I went up to her and introduced myself, but she didn't remember me. I tried to make her know me, but she just couldn't remember. I was kind of hurt; I spent every day and night with her for three months on her *first* European tour—how could she not recall? But I think Tina has blocked a lot of her past out of her mind. I guess she *had* to, just to survive. I'm glad to see her have success today. She deserves every drop of it."

This picture was taken over fifteen years ago, but today
Tina Turner is as sexy as ever. *(Michael Ochs Archives)*

Ike Turner, a guitarist, songwriter and bandleader, plucked a young Tina from her native Nutbush, Tennessee, and made her lead singer of his band. *(Michael Ochs Archives)*

Ike and Tina Turner as they looked in September 1960 while under contract to Sue Records. *(Michael Ochs Archives)*

"A Fool in Love" was Ike and Tina's very first hit record.
A young Tina, in love and making records, was on top of
the world. *(Michael Ochs Archives)*

ver a span of more than two decades, Tina's look
anged, but her beauty always remained intact.
Michael Ochs Archives)

Ike, Tina, and a version of the Ikettes, late '60s.
(Michael Ochs Archives)

One edition of Ike and Tina's backup singers, the Ikettes.
Replacements were always waiting in the wings.
(Michael Ochs Archives)

Turner, as she appeared in an early '70s publicity shot while recording for the Liberty label. *(Michael Ochs Archives)*

Ike and Tina Turner about 1970. By 1974, the hits, as well as the marriage, ended. *(Michael Ochs Archives)*

"Ike may have been in the background," Tina once said, "but he was responsible for the way the music sounded back then." *(Michael Ochs Archives)*

While many black acts were bound by the chains of
musical categories, Ike and Tina were considered a pop
act. Here, Tina appeared on the old *Sonny and Cher
Comedy Hour*. *(Michael Ochs Archives)*

Turner once confided to a photographer that she'd seldom performed without a wig during her long musical career.
(Michael Ochs Archives)

Tina has always been a raucous performer. This shot was taken in the early '70s. *(Michael Ochs Archives)*

Tina has long been accepted by rock's elite. Here she shares a laugh with Keith Richards of the Rolling Stones *(left)* and David Bowie. *(Bob Gruen/Star File Photos)*

A fan shows his appreciation. "Without the people," says
Tina, "an artist is nothing. They brought me back."
(*Anastasia Pantsios/Star File Photos*)

Few performers, male or female, can work a stage (and a mike) like Tina. *(Paul Natkin/Star File Photos)*

Ike came back to the States with a feeling of achievement, and he didn't want to let it simmer before putting it to work. Once back in Los Angeles, he huddled with associates and began orchestrating a higher visibility level for the band. Soon, Ike and Tina Turner, via mainstream shows like *Ed Sullivan* and *The Tonight Show,* were rocking suburbia, with Tina bumping, grinding and shaking her way across the dinner tables of mid-America. The only thing more humorous than watching the leggy exploits of Tina and the Ikettes work out on the fiberglass stage of the staid *Andy Williams Show* was watching the funk rocker Sly Stone of Sly and the Family Stone leave that same stage during his sixties appearance on the show and venture into the television audience, attempting, quite innocently, to prod families to "Dance to the Music." Likewise, the look on Johnny Carson's face after Ike's troupe had done its thing was just short of priceless.

Indeed, things were cooking for the Turners as they graduated from small supper clubs and began playing venues like the International Hotel in Las Vegas and huge halls like Madison Square Garden. The early sixties saw the act getting as little as $500 a night for their performances. Now, the Revue would earn as much as $20,000 for an evening's work. Not a lot of money when compared to the fees major music acts pull in today, but in the sixties it was nothing to sneeze at.

In 1969, the Rolling Stones again asked Ike and Tina to open on their concert tour, this time in the States, where the exposure for the Turners would have a direct effect. Tina recalled that while the European audiences were appreciative, the old Revue might possibly come off just a bit stale to American rock audiences, so she suggested the group learn versions of songs like the Beatles' "Come Together," Sly Stone's "I Want to Take You Higher," and Creedence Clearwater Revival's "Proud Mary," which the Turners so embraced that the song has become a musical signature for Tina Turner even today.

It was during this period that Ike, in his never-ending quest to reach mass audiences, came up with a most peculiar theory. According to an interview with *Ebony* magazine, Ike did not believe the idea held by many blacks that whites cannot "keep time" to the music. "They're on a faster rhythm than we are," he explained. "They're on the beat, but it's a double beat. This is sending out double vibrations. This," he reasoned, "is the difference between rhythm and blues and a pop sound." Whether or not that was (or is) the case, the theory certainly explained why Ike's version of "Proud Mary" always moved at breakneck speed, as did many of his covers of previously recorded material. But Ike may have had some kind of point. For the most part, Ike and Tina Turner never really caught on with young black audiences of the sixties.

In any event, Ike and Tina *had* caught on with a supportive white audience, but despite the fact that the Revue evolved into a rock and roll act, for the most part their audiences still turned to them when interested in listening to what the considered staunch R & B. At this point, any arguments on the subject were moot; Ike and Tina, along with Sly and the Family Stone, the Chambers Brothers and Billy Preston, were taken in as ardent rock 'n' soulers.

Ike, always one to alter to fit the times, jumped on the Flower Power trend with both feet. He renovated his wardrobe onstage and off, even took to wearing an afro wig on occasion. And Ike discovered something else beside mod clothing and hip lingo.

Drugs have never been a stranger to the

blues scene, Ike's origins. Back on the "chitlin' circuit," Ike had his share of problems dealing with musicians who got caught up with cocaine, alcohol and even heroin. But he never seriously took part in any of it. His only real vices were women and gambling, which, despite his talent for stretching a buck, is where his earnings sometimes went. However, in the sixties more than ever before, marijuana and more exotic drugs were being associated with musical creativity and artistic freedom. Ike wanted to be a part of it, especially if success was at the end of the experience.

In retrospect, many members of the duo's entourage reported that, more and more, Ike seemed eternally irritable. And not just about musicians being late for rehearsals or missing a note in performance. Increasingly, Ike seemed to be hassled by life itself. "Sometimes, you just didn't want to deal with him," said that ex-Ikette. "Everything had to go through Ike's consideration—he was the first and last word in that organization—and you'd find yourself learning to avoid him. For instance, if you needed expenses to be OK'd by him, sometimes you'd just absorb the cost yourself. But that was just sometimes. On other occasions, he was cool, and that's when you'd approach him."

Tina had no interest in drugs. The Turners had moved into a $100,000 home in View Park, an upscale, predominantly black suburb of Los Angeles, where such entertainers as Nancy Wilson and Ray Charles also lived. Tina was busy attempting to erect some semblance of home life, though touring still took up most of her time. Her other time she gave to her young sons—Raymond Craig and Ronnie, her own sons, and Ike Jr. and Michael from Ike's previous relationship. At first, living at home was a little disconcerting. After all, if one lives out of a suitcase most of the year, finding your toothbrush in its own stall can be an unaccustomed discovery. But Tina quickly adapted to having her own domain. After all, to be a homebody for her husband was one of her childhood dreams.

Whether because of Ike's personal taste, or just another of his interests in keeping with the times, the View Park residence was rather gaudily furnished. The colors were bright and quite often didn't coordinate with one another. In short, it was an interior decorator's nightmare. There was a huge, fancy master bedroom with mirrors on the ceiling, furniture made in the shape of various musical instruments, and keyboards and guitars all about the place, which the kids would fool around with. All of the Turner kids were coming along on guitars and piano, and their doodling sometimes got on Tina's last nerve. Tina rarely listened to music at home. In fact, Tina's interest in music began to reach a low ebb. Other than fronting it, Tina had very little creative input into the live act, and she never did any songwriting for the duo's albums. Music became strictly a job. And since it was an all-consuming job, it left her very little time to develop other interests or the opportunity for Tina to learn more about *Tina.* "I'm not into music at all," she told an interviewer during the period. "Whenever it's time to rehearse, Ike has to call me in to do it. When I'm at home, I don't even listen to [music] that much."

Ike, on the other hand, was for the most part enjoying himself. The Turners, by any standards, were now fairly wealthy and soon acquired all the trappings to suggest such. Ike drove a gleaming brown Rolls-Royce, while Tina had a white Jaguar. Ike managed to corral most of the act's money by cutting out the middleman whenever possible. His years as a hustler in the music business served him well, and he was aware of all the loopholes businessmen used to feed off an act. Today, it has become quite fashionable for an artist to maintain as much control as possible over his creative endeavors, but even in the late sixties Ike had the situation well under control.

He headed his own management company, usually served as the band's agent handling the concert bookings, and oversaw his songwriting compositions via his two music publishing companies. "Some people wanted to make us superstars overnight," Ike reasoned. "But we would have ended up with twenty-five percent of the money and they would have the rest."

4

Nowhere to Go but Up

"As for her ex-husband, Tina said she's
sure that in his own way, Ike is proud
of her accomplishments."—
Jet *magazine, 1985.*

"Naw, that ain't it . . . we'll do it again and
then come back and clean up that bass guitar
track." It's just after midnight. While most of
the business of this storefront neighborhood
called it quits long ago, the workday is just
beginning at Bolic Sound, the recording studio Ike had built in Inglewood, not far from
his Los Angeles home. Chiefly, the studio
served as the spawning ground for all Ike
and Tina Turner productions. When he
wasn't using it, it was rented out to other local recording artists and garage bands making demo tapes.

However, none of those people have been able to get in the place for three days and nights; that's how long Ike and his accompanying musicians have been holed up in here. In the main studio, cluttered by amplifiers, microphones and wiring, five musicians, including Ike, sit at their instruments wearing headphones. In three days the rhythm section has recorded the music for at least fourteen songs. Later, in a more introspective mood, Ike will attempt to write lyrics for some of this music. The guitar player misses a crucial chord more than once (Ike is playing organ), and finally Ike suggests they all take a break.

Ike heads to a little cozy loft that serves as an apartment to accommodate Ike's workaholic binges and goes for the mirror on the desk. On it is a small pile of white powder—cocaine. He takes it out into the studio and offers it to the players. Cocaine is thought by some artists to be a great tool in the studio to keep a crew of musicians going for so many hours. Ike's legendary marathon Bolic Sound sessions were fueled by cocaine, takeout chicken and pizza.

"Once, I had my wife come down and let her see for herself where I was," said one musician who participated in several of the marathon recording sessions. "She used to say, 'Ain't no way you recording no music for two days straight.' She used to think I was cheating on her. Personally, it was great for me. And people say all these things about Ike—that he was a tyrant and all this—but he was no different from any other producer working in Hollywood. He squeezed the most out of the people around him, which is the same thing Berry Gordy [chairman of Motown Records] or some movie mogul would do. Today, if you ask anyone who works for Prince or Michael Jackson, they'll tell you the same thing. Ike was just trying to get ahead, and you don't get ahead by being a weakling."

That musician's view is understandable, and others agreed that Ike's determination and concern for continued success wasn't exactly the problem. The dilemma, they insisted, was the *kind* of music he was creating during his fits of creative passion. By the seventies the music scene was changing. The Jackson Five was flourishing. Bands like the Doobie Brothers and the Ohio Players were occupying key slots on the national music charts, which suggested that pop and R & B were melding together. The Revue still had that bold soul flavor, which was fine, but to base an album on the live act was a misguided move. Ike and Tina's covers—recordings of material written and made popular by other artists—were losing their sting because, unless they ingeniously rearranged the songs, as a soul artist of the period named Isaac Hayes was doing, there was little interest. This was the age of self-containment. Ike's self-sufficient operation was missing one thing—hit records.

"I tried to tell Ike that he wasn't going to be able to do it all," said one songwriter from the period who approached Ike with compositions of his own and others. "I was interested in working with Ike and having him oversee my songwriting. You know—help me place my stuff both on his albums and with other acts. He had the setup, I had the tunes. But I think he didn't want to risk getting a hit with someone else's song. 'Proud Mary' made a lot of money—for another songwriter. When I tried to make a deal, he offered this crazy deal, including wanting to own the song himself. No way."

Up-and-coming songwriters weren't the only ones complaining of Ike's business practices. Inside United Artists, executives were getting a little concerned that Ike's well of hits might be running dry. Supposedly, cer-

tain decision makers learned the hard way—
through Ike—that a touring band doesn't always make a successful *recording* unit. The
company had some good times with the
group, but the problem as they saw it was
that the Revue wasn't performing much of its
album material live. Since the records
weren't getting much radio airplay, there was
almost no outlet for consumers to hear new
Ike and Tina material. Thus, few record
sales.

While Ike was busy at Bolic Sound trying
to come up with the duo's next hit record,
Tina was spending her days and nights in a
strange kind of void. Her relationship to Ike
by this time was almost exclusively that of
employee. She really didn't see him unless he
called her to come down to the studio to sing
on a rough track (at which time he expected
her to drop everything she was doing and be
on her way) or when he came home. However, even then he was really too submerged
in business matters to pay any real attention
to his wife. According to those who communicated with the singer at the time, this wasn't
as bad as it sounds, especially since the longer
Ike was away from home, the better chance
Tina had of not getting into trouble with
him.

Nevertheless, there was something else cutting into Tina's pride at the time, and that, according to an insider, was the fact that Ike had moved one of his girlfriends into the Turner's home. "I knew this girl," said the ex-Ikette. "She used to be an Ikette herself, when she started seeing Ike. After she stopped performing, Ike had her working, doing something else with the group. Then one day, she was just there . . . staying up there at the house. I used to wonder how she could do it, but she did. The funny thing was that Tina didn't hate the girl for it. Or at least she didn't show it. You'd call there and it would just be the two of them at the house, looking at television. But see, Tina had to take what mess Ike used to lay on her and to survive, she had to make it work for *her*. For Tina, even a woman sleeping with her man in their house served its purpose—it meant *she* didn't have to sleep with him. I think for her, that kind of interest had left a long time ago."

Amazingly, despite all of these things, Tina continued to operate as a professional. That is, she continued to work up such a sweat during her electrifying performances, that sometimes it seemed better just to discard the scanty costumes than to try to save them. Though she preferred live shows over working in the studio, she sang her heart out at Ike's command.

Certainly a highlight of Ike and Tina's spotlight in the Big Time was the Soul to Soul music festival of 1971, which took place in the West African nation of Ghana. The fifteen-hour all-night concert was designed to be part of the fourteenth independence celebration of the first sub-Saharan African nation to achieve freedom in modern times. The participants in the show—all American R & B artists—were chosen with the intent of exposing Ghanaians to the smorgasbord of American soul music.

Featured in the show was keyboard-ist/singer Les McCann, sax man Eddie Harris, the Staple Singers, Roberta Flack and the Voices of East Harlem. Despite the headlining bill of singer Wilson Pickett (touted as "Soul Brother No. 2" with due respect to James Brown), the throngs of spectators gave an especially warm reception to Ike and Tina, whose fast-paced musical revue reflected both the sexuality of the West and upbeat American soul in its most exciting form.

Tina recalled the concert, held at Black Star Square, as one of the more memorable performances of her tenure with the Revue. "I'll never forget it because I was sick with the flu or something," she said. "But it was fascinating, because oddly enough, it was our first all-black audience. It was a massive crowd and they looked like a huge black wave when they moved. When the Ikettes came on, they went wild, she laughed. "I think it was all that skin we were showing." Perhaps, but an American journalist who traveled to Africa to cover the event also reported that the festival audiences seemed to respond most to the performers who showed the most emotion and movement and ". . . the ones who screamed the most. Between Tina and Mavis Staples, they kept those folks in an uproar." During interviews with magazines and newspapers, Tina always represented the duo in a highly professional manner. In an obscure filmed documentary of the group, shot in the duo's heyday during an engagement at a Las Vegas hotel, Tina looks totally at peace, discussing her life as an entertainer with a special schoolgirl charm. Few people knew the real story.

But increasingly it was getting tougher for Tina to live the way she was living. Undoubtedly every day must have been a wild adventure of trying to get through without any

emotional upheaval. Toward the end Tina
fought to keep her sanity, but ironically, at
some point, it probably would have been better if she had lost her mind. But she still had
it, which meant she could fully discern what
was happening to her life.

In 1974, something began to happen to
Tina. More and more, when the flare-ups between her and Ike occurred, she noticed
something different. The cursing, the violent
excitement and the tears were still integral
elements of these episodes. However, with
increasing frequency, there came another
emotion—not exactly *new* by any means. But
slowly, it reared its head. When Ike would
argue and fight with Tina, her fear was being
replaced by a distinctive feeling—*anger*.

"You could feel it bottled up inside of her,"
said the ex-Ikette. "On some of those last
shows, you could see what was happening.
When she would break into something fast,
like 'Proud Mary' or 'Nutbush City Limits,'
the crowd would yell, 'Go on girl! Get
down!!' But for me, someone who did those
songs *with* her night after night, I could see
that she was putting something extra into
them. I remember her turning around toward me at one point in the song, and I
swear there was fire in her eyes. I said to

myself right then, 'Either that girl's gettin' ready to lose her mind or she's gettin' *mad*. Mad at the way she let this thing go for all these years . . . mad at Ike for doing it, but mad at herself for letting it happen. I was glad to see that look in her eyes that night, because then I knew she was gonna be all right, that she was gonna get out of this. I'll be honest with you; after that set, I got on the phone to L.A. and started looking for a new job, because I knew the Revue wasn't gonna last much longer. I knew that right then."

That Ikette was perhaps the first to witness a woman who had finally reached her limit of tolerance. The aides were the next to feel the difference in Tina. She was always a lady in dealing with aides and independent merchants associated with the Revue. While she was still an easy person to work with, she was soon quickly irritated when things weren't done to her liking. "The people who knew what she was going through understood," said the ex-Ikette. "Some people had known what Ike was puttin' down long before even *Tina* in some cases. So, they worked with her."

However, Ike himself was to get a taste of Tina's anxiety firsthand. The straw that broke Tina's emotional back came later in

1974 while the duo was back on the road. According to members of the entourage, the chain of events began when Ike erupted into one of his spasms of physical violence while on a plane en route to a concert date in Dallas. The incident was nothing out of the norm—Ike slapped Tina while sitting in the first-class section. But members of the Revue noticed that *this* time, Tina disputed Ike in their argument. "I don't really know what they were fighting about," said one musician who was in the entourage at the time. He said a stewardess working the flight, aware that he was part of the Turner party, informed him of the incident in case she had to call on him to cool Ike down. "She kept telling me fighting wasn't allowed on the plane and that if anything went down, she'd have to get the captain. I couldn't think about anything but Tina holding her own. It wasn't a big scene or anything. If you were nearby, you wouldn't have known anything was happening. I couldn't hear what Tina was saying, but I saw the look on her face and how she was looking at Ike. That was something new."

According to Tina's account of that same episode, in a 1984 cover story in *Rolling Stone* magazine, the fight continued even after they got off the plane in Dallas. "When I got in the car," she told interviewer Kurt Loder, "he gave me a backhand, just like that. And I remember pointing my finger in his face and saying, 'I told you. You got the money, you got everything. I'm gonna try to stay—but I'm not gonna take your licks anymore.' And then the big fight started—and I started hitting back. I didn't cry once. I cursed back and I yelled, and he goes, 'You son of a bitch, you never talked to me like this before.' And I said, 'That's right, but I am now!'"

Tina went on to say that when the car arrived at the hotel, "My face was swollen out past my ear. Blood was everyplace." Amazingly, despite what had just happened, Tina immediately reverted to what Ike expected of her. When the fervor calmed, she said she began massaging his head, and showing the usual concern for his comfort. But this fight had a different ending. "He went and laid across the bed," Tina told *Rolling Stone*, "and he started snoring. And I leaned over and I said . . . goodbye."

Tina had less than 50 cents when she walked out of the hotel suite. She contacted actress Ann-Margret, whom she'd met during her brief appearance in the 1975 rock film *Tommy;* the actress wired Tina a plane ticket from L.A. As Ike lay across the king-sized bed in slumber, his wife, distraught but free once and for all, was on a plane back to Los Angeles. For the first time in almost sixteen years, Tina, during a flight that undoubtedly seemed to take days, made up her mind that from that day forward, Tina would live life for *Tina*. It was hard to break away from the fear. She once told a friend that even though she knew it was physically impossible, she felt that when she stepped off that plane, somehow Ike would be there, ready to assault her once more.

What power, after almost two decades, finally forced her to leave Ike? As she told one magazine reporter years after her freedom flight, "I had taken about as much physical and emotional abuse as I could handle. There is nothing complicated about it. It's possible to push a person too far, and I was pushed beyond the limit."

Once in Los Angeles, Tina was afraid to return to their home; she accepted the invitation from Ann-Margret, and took refuge at her home, where she stayed for six months. When Ike finally awakened from his nap back in Dallas, he experienced a feeling he hadn't encountered very often in his musical career. For the first time since Art Lassiter stood him up during the recording of "A Fool in Love" at the Revue's inception, Ike found himself without a backup. Ike canceled many plans that day—the night's performance, the other dates behind it. That dark day in Dallas, Ike canceled his future. For once in sixteen years, he could not control what was happening to him.

5

A New Beginning

"Everyone said, 'When are you going to grow up? When are you going to put on a wonderful dress and a fur?' It just was not me, I just had too much energy. I just stuck to what I wanted."—Tina in an interview with **Jet** *magazine, 1985.*

"Anytime there's a separation or divorce," said Tina, "there's a change, with possibilities for a whole new life in whatever direction you take it." That is the thought that fueled Tina's emotional resurrection. For sixteen years, she existed as someone's virtual puppet, and she needed something optimistic to have as her theme through the maze that would bring her back to control her life.

The first year that Tina was separated from Ike, she did nothing. She wouldn't think about music. The thought of it made her sick. She didn't care who was number one on the charts. When the radio was on, she often turned it off. "I needed not to think about it," she said of the period. "Music was my life—a bad chapter in my life. I didn't want to be reminded of it, and that's what music did."

Without music, Tina found that she was virtually a nonperson. For once in her life she didn't have to think about what she was going to wear at the Felt Forum, Hollywood Palladium or the Spectrum in Philadelphia. There was no need to scout the radio looking for a new tune to rearrange and make her own. For the first time in years, she didn't have to concern herself with the petty disagreements that went on among the Ikettes, musicians and other people who surrounded her, many of whom she didn't even like.

"It was kinda hard at first," said a friend who kept tabs on Tina while the singer stayed with a mutual friend. "I think deep down she might have been wondering who would really help her out. When something like this happens, you really find out who your friends are. In a business like hers, when you're on top you've got plenty of friends. There wasn't anything glamorous about what she was going through. She didn't have any money, and to some people, once she walked out on Ike, the fame was gone, too. I'm sure she worried about that. It's one thing to ask for a couple of dollars to tide you over; it's another thing altogether when you have to ask someone to hide you from your husband. She never had to count on anybody in that way. She was wondering if they'd be there."

More importantly, Tina needed something to replenish her peace of mind, or as that friend put it, "She needed to be able to focus on something. When it was clear that her mind was open to something new, that's when things began to happen." For Tina, that something turned out to be Buddhism. In the late seventies the religion had begun to catch on, especially among Hollywood's show business crowd. The Buddhist practice of meditation and chanting of a "mantra," or mystical, non-discursive word or words, moves one out of ordinary forms of thought and into a state of enlightened consciousness. Several top-chart recording artists swore by its results. Tina's supporters introduced her to the idea of chanting long before she left Ike, and she had begun practicing it as often as she could with what she felt were incredible results. Having been raised in the Baptist church, Tina was cautious when she was first exposed to chanting, because she had associated it with witchcraft. "I tested it," she told *Ebony* magazine. "I had gone shopping and overspent. I just knew Ike would kill me, so I chanted about it. then he called me into the studio and said, 'Come and sing this song.' I just sang it so perfectly that he looked in a drawer and pulled out a wad of money and said, 'Here, go shopping.' After that, I said, 'It works! I don't care what anybody says, I'm doing it.' And I've been doing it ever since. I just think that chanting puts you on a different frequency and helps you get what you want faster—happiness, good health, material things, whatever."

Tina had a lot to chant for. With no income whatsoever, she had to think about feeding herself, as well as about the welfare of her children, who for the moment remained with Ike.

In the meantime, Ike was suffering his own share of woes. Those closer to him said Ike all but went to pieces in the first days of the separation. The immediate problem was the fact that he had an operation to run, people to pay, deadlines and commitments and a band with no lead singer. There were also reports that Ike was deeper into the drug scene than anyone really knew.

"Believe me, Tina wasn't the only person having it hard," said a source close to Ike who requested anonymity. "Ike was going crazy. See, the main thing for him is that *nobody,* especially Tina, had ever gotten fed up with this thing and told him where to go. It was a trip. At first, it was anger. You'd go by the pad and Tina's name would come up. It was almost if he was going to bite your head off for mentioning her, but then he wanted to talk about it. I guess kind of reason out. 'What's she gon' do? Where's she gon' go? How's she gonna get a band together? She can't do nothing without me. She'll be back.' It was that kind of thing. There must have been another side that was weeping inside, but he never let me see it."

Inevitably, when she built up the courage, Tina had to communicate with Ike. there were, after all, things to be taken care of. Most importantly, she wanted to try to explain to him exactly why she had walked out on him, even though to even distant associates, the answer was clear. There were the kids, the house and personal effects that Tina needed. However, whenever she called, she got an earful of hostility, threats and confusion. "I was at the studio once while he was having a conversation with her," the source close to Ike said. "The conversation on his part started out real cold and calm, but pretty soon, he was heated. You never heard such language. And at the top of his lungs. Her ear must have fallen off after a while. She hung up on him and then we [the people there at the studio] had to listen to this stuff for about an hour." According to the source, Ike's plan was to ". . . allow things to get so bad for Tina that she'd come crawling back." They'd heard that Tina, in order to meet day-to-day expenses, had applied for public assistance. "Somebody said something about food stamps," the source hinted. "I don't know."

Around the end of 1976, Tina came to the conclusion that suffering in the wake of her past would only mean slow death. Life as an entertainer is all she'd ever known, but according to those close to her during the period, Tina seriously considered doing something else for a living. "The fear that she would fail was certainly there," said a friend. "She'd worked under the wing of someone else for so long—her career was molded by someone else—that she didn't know if she could do it. That's where the chanting came in. Having that to give her strength really helped."

So it was clear: Tina Turner would carry on as a solo act. In the meantime, she had also filed for divorce from Ike. While the legalities were being finalized, Tina had to avoid the man. Verbal abuse became the norm, and when he finally found out where Tina lived, he thought nothing of attempting to drop in on her unexpectedly. There was one report of bullets being fired into her residence, and a friend confided that for a while, Tina had taken to carrying a gun herself.

With her mind made up to continue performing, Tina consulted with several music business connections, all of whom advised her that the best way to get back into the groove was to hit the Las Vegas lounge circuit. She went to work gathering a band and secretly went into rehearsals. "Once I got back in front of a band, the electricity was there immediately," she has said. "Entertaining is what I *do,* simple as that. Once I got back up there, I knew that I couldn't do anything else. That is my world up there."

Tina's hastily assembled camp of advisors may have been correct about Vegas, but her own instincts told her the best place to begin her journey back into the spotlight was to go back to Europe, where she and Ike had enjoyed their biggest success. She and her small band covered the continent, hitting all the major cities. The tour marked the beginning of a love affair between the artist and Europe that continues to this day. "An appreciative audience is an appreciative audience anywhere," Tina said, "but there's something about the European audiences. The first time I ever really remember receiving an encore was in Europe. Their roar was so different; it was the kind of thing where you actually had to ask, 'Is all this noise for me?' It was great."

Still, Tina's resurrection was in the embryonic stage. By 1978, her divorce was final. The good news was that after sixteen years Tina was free to live her life again. The bad news was that the court deemed her walking out on the marriage a bad business move. Thus, Tina became heir to bills and other financial commitments incurred as Ike and Tina Turner. When promoters and agents finished hitting her up for all the engagements cancelled as a result of her flight in the middle of a concert tour, the total came to thousands. "There was a lot to live down," Tina said in a 1984 interview. "Not just paying back financial commitments, but just in the way some people were treated by Ike during the early years. There were people I found myself having to deal with, years later, all over again. But many of those people—agents and promoters—were good to me. They respected the situation I was in, they helped."

Nevertheless, the road was rough. Compared to the Ike and Tina days, the new Tina tours were done on a shoestring. No more five-star hotels. As opposed to flying from date to date, as she and Ike often did, Tina and band were busing it. The irony was that many critics had always considered Ike and Tina, even at the height of their success, a glorified lounge act that managed to garner mass acceptance. And here Tina was, years later—after Phil Spector, after Johnny Carson, after making a name for herself on the "A" list of show-biz figures (Ronald Reagan probably knew who Tina Turner was long before he became President of the United States and long before "What's Love Got to Do with It") and generating over a million dollars in the process—actually working her lounge act in Vegas *lounges*.

However, years later, even Tina admitted to having worked the circuit of dying artists when she first resurrected her music career. "Let's just say we weren't exactly playing the MGM Grand Hotel [in Las Vegas] in the beginning," said one musician who played with Tina. "They weren't really dumps . . . well, some of them were pretty funky. That was the name of the game at the time. She had to go through the same stuff that club owners and agents pull on sixteen-year-olds doing their first gig away from their father's garage. Some of the lighting and sound arrangements were just ridiculous. Then, every now and then some smartass would try to tack all these unheard of expenses onto her fee and not pay what he promised. Some of these cats figured, "This chick ain't going nowhere; we can treat her any kind of way, and she's happy just for the gigs.' I have to respect her guts. I'll be honest with you—it was just a gig for me; I *never* thought she'd break out of those doldrums. I figured she'd end up on somebody's rock and roll oldies show."

The fact is, Tina's own show, in the beginning, wasn't much different from what she used to do with Ike. Some standards, like "Proud Mary" (which is still part of her set today) and "River Deep–Mountain High," couldn't be left out. Except, perhaps, for the order in which the songs were delivered, Tina didn't touch too much of anything. "I saw her years later, on her own at the Country Club in Los Angeles," said Michele Elyzabeth. "It was the very same show I'd seen her do years ago when I worked for her and Ike. It was kind of sad. You could see that some of the people [in the audience] were there for nostalgia's sake."

Ultimately, once Tina came to realize that her artistic and financial destinies were in her own hands, that she was the only person between the show sinking or swimming, she altered the set to a glitzy, almost Saturday Night Feverish proportion, with male and female dancers and covers of dance tunes.

"She was trying to keep pace with the times," explained the musician who accompanied Tina during the period, "but I think the problem was that she wasn't following her heart. Even back with Ike, the stuff was more rock-oriented. It was R & B, but the energy was clearly rock and roll, I'd say. That was the problem back then. She was just trying to come up with a show that would get her bookings. It's like Chuck Berry playing Mozart, when he really wants to be jamming 'Lucille.'"

6

Tina Turner the Burner

"Tina does not smother a song in lip gloss; she slams into a song with megatons of natural energy. It's almost crass, but somehow it seems to work."—**The Face** *magazine, 1984.*

By the late seventies, Tina Turner was back in the groove. Now a solo act, she had turned the operation into a well-oiled machine reminiscent of the Revue and drove it with Ike's intensity. The gigs were there—she was still a big enough name to get dates in Vegas, Europe and middle America. And the money wasn't bad. Even though the bills incurred from her tormented past took their share, she still knocked the total down.

Her personal life was beginning to blossom as well. Now more than ever, she relied on her chanting sessions—"nam-myo-ho-renge-kyo, nam-myo-ho-renge-kyo, nam-myo-ho-renge-kyo"—to keep her life in order. Such mystic sounds, or mantra, are believed by Buddhists to be sonic representations of reality, and chanting such sounds can bring reality into being. It was working in more ways than one, as weekly meetings with other Buddhists often allowed her to replenish her ailing social life. "You can understand," said the ex-Ikette, "how difficult it was to get back into the swing of things. Men have a way of allowing you to hate them. That sounds rough, but once Tina was out of her marriage, slowly, the things came out. She'd want to talk about it over dinner or something, at times when you think she'd rather leave it alone. Finally, she started trusting people again." Tina hadn't entirely given up on relationships, but it would be difficult. After all, the woman spent half her life on the road paying for one bad relationship. "She didn't want to make the same mistake twice," said the Ikette. "It's possible, you know."

Finally, Tina knew the kind of man she wanted. "I just don't want to be depended on any longer," she would say. "I have men friends, but I'm not going steady with anyone now. It's hard to go steady unless you drag him along with you on the road, and

I'm not into dragging anyone with me right now." However, it was apparent that Tina's own personal desires and concepts of home life—if not marriage—had not been totally fulfilled during her relationship with Ike. "I like strong men," she said. "I'm a little old-fashioned. A man must be a man, but he must allow me my freedom and respect. But what's most important is that he must be strong."

Perhaps today she was having second thoughts about the situation, but as late as age forty-two, Tina was sharing with friends the fact that she wanted to have another child within the next few years. "It would be a girl," she told *Ebony*. "My psychic reader has already told me. If I got pregnant now," she said at the time, "even without a husband, I would have the child. I've already talked to my doctor about it, and he says I'm fine."

Fate obviously had something else in store for her, but even Tina knew there was more she wanted to accomplish. By now she was recovering from the early years, but she was still considered a has-been by show business standards. During these times, she huddled with Richard Perry, producer of such artists as the Pointer Sisters and Diana Ross. He expressed an interest in producing her solo album, but it simply resulted in some forgettable tracks. "I'm hard to capture on tape, if I must say so myself," Tina said years later. "I'd much rather do it live. In the beginning, you just go in there and sing. Today, you've got all the high technology. You're out there in that studio alone without a band and it seems like a thousand miles away from civilization. And then you have to wear those headphones and they keep falling off. I believe I can sing anything, but it's hard to come up with the right song to capture the feelings in my voice. I've done some good stuff in the past, but I don't know if my best was *ever* captured on tape."

After Perry's project struck out (he had similarly tepid results with singer Martha Reeves earlier), the record companies figured there was nothing left of the Tina Turner legend, and her search for recording contracts were met with cold feet. Usually their ploy was to suggest that Tina come up with some hot tracks for their consideration, but as Tina has said, "the combination has to be right," and it never was, although every now and then some questionable R & B producer would tell her he could revive her career. Of course today everyone feels differently about Tina. "I would have loved to have her here," said one Warner Brothers Records exec, just after "What's Love Got to Do with It" hit the number one spot on the charts. "I was mentioning to some people here what Tina could do. I told them, 'She's gonna surface somewhere. Why don't we try it?' Personally, I would have teamed her with Prince [also a Warners artist]. At the time, I think the company was thinking of the problems they had with Sly Stone. Warners spent a lot of money trying to bring his career around and nothing happened. I couldn't convince them that Tina's situation was different. First of all, we weren't talking about a drug problem but an identity crisis. I know a million A & R men [artist and repertoire people are responsible for finding and signing new acts for a record company] have said it now, but I knew Tina Turner just needed a hit record. Everything else was there."

The powers at major record labels weren't the only ones who weren't sure of Tina's ability to bounce back. Unfortunately, even the associates in her own camp seemed to harbor apprehensions. They seemed privately content to keep Tina on the performing circuit, even though she expressed more and more interest in doing other things. "My goals seemed so far away about five years ago that I didn't share them with very many people," Tina has said. "My plan has been to work in all areas of entertainment. I had hopes of that, even with Ike. Unfortunately, everyone doesn't always see your abilities as you see your own."

Tina continued to make alterations in her act. To spice up her visual presentation, she added background singer/dancers Ann Behringer and LeJune Richardson, who added more sex appeal as well as movement to the set. But something was still missing. She hired a rock band to work behind her. That helped, but when Tina turned her attention to what really bothered her, she knew exactly what she had to do. "I needed people around me who felt the same way I did about my career," she said. "I needed people working on my behalf who felt that I could go all the way. I didn't need anyone on my team working against me."

Tina quickly came to the conclusion that she needed a manager. Not just someone to help her count her money; she'd had enough of not being in total control of her life, personally, financially and professionally. What she needed was someone with vision, aspiration and creative planning ability. She

One of Tina's key comeback moves was to open the 1984 sell-out concerts of Lionel Richie. *(Paul Natkin/Star File Photos)*

Tina doing what she does best, performing onstage.
(Bob Gruen/Star File Photos)

Tina doesn't just sing a song—she attacks it.
(Anastasia Pantsios/Star File Photos)

A rare moment, Tina quiet behind a microphone.
(Anastasia Pantsios/Star File Photos)

Chatting with an unidentified fan.
(Bob Gruen/Star File Photos)

"I was always a rocker," Tina has said, as she and the
Stones' Keith Richards strike a jubilant pose.
(Bob Gruen/Star File Photos)

Tina and Keith Richards backstage in Europe.
(Bob Gruen/Star File Photos)

Tina backstage at the Ritz with Susan Sarandon, David Bowie, Keith Richards, and John McEnroe. *(Bob Gruen/Star File Photos)*

Two cultural giants: Tina Turner and the Eiffel Tower in Paris. *(Bob Gruen/Star File Photos)*

In spite of her ultrasexy image, Tina has never been branded simply as a sex object. Here she poses with a crew of Playboy Bunnies. *(Paul Natkin/Star File Photos)*

"If anyone goes away displeased from my show," says
Tina, "it wasn't because I didn't give my all."
(Anastasia Pantsios/Star File Photos)

"I love performing, but in the back of my mind, I've always wanted to be a housewife." *(Anastasia Pantsios/Star File Photos)*

Tina: "I'll keep doing what I'm doing until my body tells me to slow down." *(Anastasia Pantsios/Star File Photos)*

A jubilant Turner clowns for photographers at the 1984 MTV Awards. *(Chuck Pulin/Star File Photos)*

I hear music: Tina entertains photographers with two of the three Grammys she won at the 1985 ceremony. *(Attila Csupo)*

"What's Love Got to Do with It"? In the case of this American Music Award, everything. *(Attila Csupo)*

Tina playfully kisses one of her Grammys. *(Attila Csupo)*

Tina stalking off with yet another American Music Award. *(Attila Csupo)*

Tina accepting one of the many bouquets given in celebration of her stunning musical comeback in 1984. *(Bob Leafe/Star File Photos)*

The sure smile of a triumphant woman. *(Attila Csupo)*

needed someone who would listen to her career plans and not cringe when she voiced goals that seemed light-years away.

The best way to find management like that, Tina figured, was to look at an artist who was doing the things that Tina had in mind for her own career. The manager also had to be someone who wouldn't give her the rap that she should first become an R & B star before tackling the broader entertainment world. Thus the manager had to be someone who wasn't accustomed to funneling his acts to pop stardom that way. Tina focused on the career of Olivia Newton-John. Olivia seemed to have the best of all worlds. She made records, and most importantly, she made those recordings between major movie roles. Tina had wanted to concentrate on acting from her early days with Ike. "When I was young, I used to play like I was a star. I was always singing and dancing, but mostly I thought of myself as a *movie* star. I looked at television all the time, but we didn't even own a record player when I met Ike."

In 1981, Tina invited Lee Kramer, who directed the career of Newton-John, to see one of her shows at San Francisco's Fairmont Hotel. At this time, Tina was still doing the neo-disco lounge act with her band attired in tuxedos. She and her background singer/dancers were wearing middle American sexiness—revealing sequined outfits. Kramer was accompanied by an Australian assistant, a man named Roger Davies. They checked out Tina's show, and while Kramer saw potential, he must have figured that transforming Tina from a lounge act to an eighties rock and roll act would take more than a little doing. Apparently, in his conversations with the artist, he didn't perceive that mentally Tina was already there. The show he saw—the tip of an iceberg that had been performing two shows a night, six days a week, in America's hotel ballrooms and convention centers for months on end—was simply a way to garner enough money for Tina to make a down payment on her future.

It was ironic. Tina had chosen Kramer for his creative vision, but his lack of it turned out to be the career break his assistant Davies was looking for. To be sure, Roger Davies was as put off by the glitz of Tina's show as Kramer was, but under those sequined outfits and supper-club antics, he obviously saw something special. Apparently, he felt the *energy* of Tina's show. It was the same energy that fueled Tina's onstage duet with Mick

Jagger during a torrid rendition of the Stones' "Honky Tonk Woman," years ago. This was the same woman who, during the taping of a TV Christmas special in England three years before, had the Eurhythmics' Annie Lennox in the wings singing and dancing right along with her.

Once Kramer made it officially clear that he'd pass on the Turner proposal, Davies didn't try to persuade him otherwise. He simply finished up his duties at Kramer's company and began conducting meetings of his own with the singer. "I think we were on the same wavelength from the very beginning," Tina would later relate. "When I would tell him of my ideas, he could understand exactly what I was talking about. He also had some ideas of his own that I liked. But the main thing is, when I suggested things, he wanted to help me get it done instead of telling me I couldn't do it." (In the beginning, Davies had a partner—Chip Lightman. Lightman would later vacate the scene as well, leaving Davies alone to manage Turner's affairs.)

Turner and Davies, having joined forces, were both impatiently excited about their new union, but things had to change gradually. Tina couldn't just drop out of her present situation—she learned the hard way about not keeping commitments. She kept the conventions and supper-club dates; they paid the bills.

Slowly Turner and Davies began rebuilding Turner's career. The first order of things was to reconstruct the act. They didn't want to alienate the polyester crowd at those conventions, but unless those people had been on another planet for the last thirty years, surely they'd heard rock and roll before. And, even with the old Tina Turner show, the action and music onstage wasn't exactly Lawrence Welk. To set off favorites like "Proud Mary" and "River Deep–Mountain High," Turner threw in rock tunes from the current Top 40. After helping her update the act, Davies went to work seeking a recording contract for his client. That was the only way to get off the lounge circuit merry-go-round once and for all.

Now more than ever, Ike Turner seemed like he was on the other side of the world. He still would fall into a fit of anger every now and then and try to reach Tina on the phone to give her a piece of his mind, but for the most part, Tina was flying free of his burden. Sources from the period said Ike scoured through his studio masters and tried to make a deal on old Ike and Tina tracks with K-Tel and the Kent label, but, according to associates, Ike spent a lot of time thinking about the past. "We'd have a drink, and the conversation would always turn to the Revue days," said one associate. "Then he would talk about what he could have done had Tina not walked out on him. 'I was gonna give her whatever she wanted, but she couldn't handle it,' he used to say. But I don't really think even Ike believed Tina would survive out there. When he would talk about what he was going to do for her, it was like he felt she would be out there playing those small gigs forever. When 'What's Love Got to Do with It' made her a big star, he had to be as surprised as anyone else."

In the meantime, while pursuing a record deal, Davies once again turned to Europe, which always seemed to be the spawning ground for Tina's biggest successes. Once there, Turner again plugged into more live dates. Then, in 1982, Heaven 17, an English synthesizer pop band, invited Tina to perform on a production they were working on in the studio. Tina heard a bit of the band's music and agreed to help them out. The song was something she was familiar enough with—a rendition of "Ball of Confusion," a

Norman Whitfield composition recorded and made a hit in 1970 by the Temptations. The track, a battery of rhythmic synthesizers, came to life when Tina put her raucous pipes on it. The record wasn't an absolute smash, but more importantly for Tina, it proved that she had what it took to work in the eighties music scene. "That was the beginning of something," she said three years later. "The sound, the beat—it was *today*. It was the direction I was interested in moving in. It felt good to hear my voice on something so contemporary."

A year later Tina would begin to reach her stride. By now she had begun to tailor the act to accommodate the venue she was playing. At the Ritz, a hip New York City music spot, she would let loose with an all-rock show. Even the sets in convention ballrooms were exuding their own kind of electricity; at least enough so that word had gotten around in pop music circles: "Something's happening with Tina. Things are getting ready to pop."

Thus, when she was in her dressing room at the Ritz preparing for the show, she couldn't help noticing Davies pacing back and forth nervously. "He kept saying things like 'Darling, is everything all right?'" Tina told reporter David Thomas of *The Face*. "I knew then something was going on." After the show, in the dressing room, Davies let the cat out of the bag: "He said, 'Guess who's here—Keith Richards and David Bowie.' I just started screaming and pictures were taken and it looked as though we were having a party, but there was no one else in the room except us! I don't like to know when anyone is in the audience because when I do, it gets to me—I forget a line or something. But it was so good to see these people!"

Their makeshift party went well into the night, with Richards carrying on at the piano and the Stones' Ronnie Wood dropping by and playing some guitar. "All the while Keith kept saying, 'I'll find you a hit—we've got thousands of tracks we've never used. Do you want to come to Paris tomorrow? We'll cut some tracks.' I said, 'Keith, we're in the middle of a tour,' but he just went, 'Come on over anyway—no one will mind.'"

The scene that night at the Ritz rekindled Tina's spirit. She knew Richards and Bowie came by to encourage her. Despite their huge individual successes, they'd both experienced their share of droughts in their careers. (Indeed, Bowie's 1983 single "Let's Dance" rescued his career from the doldrums, while the Rolling Stones have certainly endured enough dips and peaks to know that popularity is not immortal.) It was important that Tina now feel like a part of the rock and roll community instead of a mere spectator. In any event, the good fortune that was to come for Tina would, if not overshadow the accomplishments of her comrades, certainly thrust her into their superstar league once and for all.

7

The Making of a Superstar

"Give me a boy and I'll give you [back] a man."—Tina Turner's line as the Acid Queen in the rock musical Tommy.

In 1983, Michael Jackson was crowned king of the pop music world. His monumental solo album, *Thriller,* had sold a little more than thirty million copies. Unquestionably, it was an accomplishment that put Jackson in a class by himself. But '83 was also the year that Tina Turner would begin her quest to be crowned queen of rock. Roger Davies had firmed up a deal for Tina to record for Capitol Records' London division. It wasn't the States, but it was a beginning. Well aware of the success Tina enjoyed in Europe during her Revue days, he figured a record over there would at least allow his client to gain even more longevity on the touring circuit.

When it came time to record her first single of the Capitol deal, Tina knew it had to be something very "eighties." She and Davies decided that perhaps she should go back to Heaven 17 members Greg Walsh and Martyn Ware, who produced the "Ball of Confusion" track. "I thought of a lot of people," Tina said, "but I enjoyed working with them, and sometimes that's more important than being a genius."

Walsh and Ware were absolutely flattered when Tina came to them for a song. "She came to us and asked whether we would write a single for her, because she'd liked working with us on *Music of Quality and Distinction,* recalled Ware. "We said yes and then realized that we wouldn't have time to write anything properly."

So the two producers looked around for a song they'd like to work with, something that Tina would agree to as well. What they ended up with was "Let's Stay Together," a mid-tempo soul standard written and made famous by souler Al Green. Tina's new career was so valiantly structured to be rock and roll–based that it was ironic that Walsh and Ware would suggest pure R & B. "But

I'd always loved that song," said Tina. "I used to sing it around the house. I thought it was the kind of tune that transcended any barriers. Anyone could sing that song. So, we went in and did it."

According to Ware, the two, in their brief time working as professionals in the world of pop music, had never encountered what Tina gave. "She was brilliant," he said, "astonishing to work with. Totally professional—a different class from anything we'd been involved with. Every note she sang was as it should be. We usually have to go through stuff endlessly, correcting it note by note, but she just seems to know exactly what is needed and does it. We got in the first or second take. We did three or four just for luck, but they were all brilliant."

"Let's Stay Together," with Walsh and Ware adding background vocals, was then released as a single in Britain. Almost immediately, Tina found herself with a Top 10 smash in the U.K. Ultimately, the record earned Tina a Silver Disc Award, accounting for sales in excess of 250,000. The success of the record demanded a major European tour, which sold out in every port. Suddenly Tina Turner found herself with a hit.

Capitol, which had taken a passing interest

in the idea of Tina's recording "Let's Stay Together," decided to release the single in the United States. The results were pretty much the same—Tina's record scored high on the charts—number five on the national R & B charts and number one on the dance charts. Executives at Capitol's Hollywood headquarters were flabbergasted. "See, they thought Tina was washed up," said an executive who worked on the Tina Turner project but has since moved on to another label. "Everyone was walking around with their head up their behinds when Tina's record was released here. I kept telling them, 'I think we've got something here. When this thing explodes, is our force gonna be ready for it?' They just sorta yawned. When the record took off, it almost didn't happen. They almost lost the album and everything."

Whether that's true or not, the success *did* surprise everyone involved—Roger Davies, Capitol, Walsh and Ware, and especially Tina. "I'll be the first to admit it," she said. "We did the record one day and the next thing I know, we've got a big record. It was exciting, but kinda scary at the same time." Capitol, determined to make the most of a good thing, allotted Turner and Davies a budget of $150,000 to go into the studio and put together an album. That was the good news. The bad news was that they had only two weeks to do it. "It was crazy," laughed Tina of the predicament in 1983. "Here we were in the middle of a major tour, and trying to do an album. *In two weeks.* Since the single caught us with our pants down, so to speak, you can imagine what we had pulled together—nothing. Roger started looking around for songs and would introduce them to me while we were in the midst of the tour. We were running around like chickens with our heads cut off."

Not surprisingly, when Davies let word out that he needed songs and producers for the Turner project, able bodies came running out of the woodwork. However, the interesting fact—which ultimately gave the work its peculiar, fresh sound—was that those hired were basically New Music advocates. There were no "name" producers involved. When contacted, Rupert Hine, songwriter and producer for an English band called the Fixx, came up with "I Might Have Been Queen," a song he composed specifically for Tina. Heaven 17 were invited to participate (Let's Stay Together" ended up on the album as well), and decided to produce a rendition of David Bowie's "1984." Mark Knopfler of the group Dire Straits brought his whole band in to cut his song, a tune called "Private Dancer" which was originally to be included on a Straits album. Finally, Davies inducted one of his Australian countrymen, Terry Britten, who brought with him a song he had cowritten called "What's Love Got to Do with It." When she heard it, Tina knew immediately she didn't like it.

"Roger had set up a meeting with me and Terry," she reflected, "and he was a nice guy. Kinda shy. He told me that when he writes a song, he just writes it but then tailors it to what the particular singer might need. Well, when I heard 'What's Love Got to Do with It,' I just didn't like it. I just didn't feel it was *me*. Roger said, 'Well, don't be so hasty; give it some time.' But I didn't like it. After I'd heard it, though, Terry got on the guitar and we just started working with it, right there. The demo tape he played for me was just too soft. By the time he finished it, it was much more rough. Sometimes you hear a song immediately, sometimes you don't. Roger heard it right off. It took me some time."

Britten produced his song; so did the others. In the end, it would add to the individuality of each song, which collectively, would add to the project's overall unique sound.

Tina also garnered the services of rock guitarist extraordinaire Jeff Beck, a longtime admirer who was seen in the front row of a couple of Tina's sold-out European dates. "Jeff—what can I say about this man?!" Tina exclaimed. "He's just an incredible guitarist. He's also a shy kind of guy. I hung around the studio for the first few solos he put on 'Private Dancer' and [the track] 'Steel Claw'; he came up with some great stuff, but he kept insisting he could do better. I said 'All right, but I'm gonna go get something to eat. Do what you will, but just save the takes that I like.' When I got back, he had laid down some great licks. At the end of the session he pulled out this new pink guitar he had and took a knife and asked me to scratch my name into it."

There was another track cut for the album that would become *Private Dancer* that was never released on the American version—a rendition of the Beatles' "Help!" The song was produced by the pop-jazz group the Crusaders, who just happened to be in London when the Turner project was coming together. "That was something," said Tina, "because those guys obviously had something else in mind when we went into the studio, and it came out sounding different. In the end, we were all happy with the results. They're great guys."

Unbelievably, in the whirlwind period of two weeks, Tina and company finished *Private Dancer* and continued their European tour. It was an incredible feat, from album cover photo to the final tracks, all completed and turned over to Capitol.

The label thought it was time for Tina to meet the press regarding her latest accomplishment, so she began huddling with newspaper and magazine reporters. Turner and Davies' plan thus far had worked. The next step was to let the world know exactly where she was headed. So Tina talked *an awful lot* about being a rocker, of her interest in performing rock music, of her associations with people like Rod Stewart and the Rolling Stones. The idea was to have Tina embraced not solely as an R & B singer but as a pop artist.

By the time Tina and Davies pulled into Los Angeles, Capitol had yet to release the *Private Dancer* LP. while "Let's Stay Together" was indeed a hit record, for the most part the major press corps was not impressed. A company publicist got on the phone and rounded up enough journalists and reporters to fill the conference room at

Capitol's circular Vine Street skyscraper. Some of the journalists admitted the real reason they showed up for the noontime conference was that the publicist mentioned something about sandwiches, juice and an assortment of pastries. "Let's face it," said one reporter. "Tina Turner? She's washed up. I figured, what the hell; if I can come into Hollywood, take care of some business and get lunch too, it was a pretty good deal." Other writers and photographers, while not as bold in their admissions, clearly weren't excited about the prospect of being in the room with Tina Turner. Some of these people were the same ones who packed into the conference room over at CBS Records a year ago, just to get a fleeting glimpse of Michael Jackson as he received an award from Jane Fonda, honoring *Thriller*'s hitting the three million mark in sales.

However, there was a pocket of journalists at the Turner conference who recognized the privilege here. They represented Europe and Japan, places where Tina had been heralded as a superstar without a hit record.

After a video of "Let's Stay Together," featuring Tina lip-synching the song and executing Revue-ish choreography with her two female dancers (who were later dropped because they were too reminiscent of the Ikette days), a publicity person announced that Tina had arrived. The European contingent applauded, while the scavengers put away their sandwiches. Tina Turner walked in the room on those long legs in leopardskin pumps and ended everything. She looked like a *star!* The tousled, dark reddish brown mane and lithe, leather-clad frame stopped traffic—and idle conversation. Immediately her presence commanded respect. She asked for nothing. "Good morning," she cheerfully issued to no one in particular as she made her way to a table cluttered with microphones and tape recorders. To those observing her there, it was hard to believe this was the same woman who had gone through years of anguish and torment. She had revamped and regrouped. Totally. For the next hour and a half, Tina spoke eloquently on all facets of her life, personal and professional, although when queried on the subject of leisure hobbies, she hesitated, then said, "Management suggested to me that I keep some things a secret, and I agree with that." She seemed to interpret the question to ask if she had a boyfriend. That question never materialized.

One reporter preceded his question with a

rather lengthy, patronizing put-down of Ike. Tina listened intently and then before answering the question, politely but firmly put the reporter in his place. "Let me correct you," she said. "Ike played a key role in my development as an entertainer. While I was up there singing and dancing, he was dealing with a lot back there. And no, he wasn't mute. He simply had me and the Ikettes doing what he would have, had he been able to sing and dance."

The questions went on and on until finally the publicist interrupted, informing the room that Tina was on a tight schedule. While an advance cassette of "What's Love Got to Do with It," blared in the background, reporters huddled around Tina, and photographers took last-minute shots. That hungry reporter who showed up only for lunch was at Tina's side, insisting that she take a picture with him. It was clear that Tina had captured the whole room.

The next stage of Davies' star plan for Tina was to expose her to audiences in the United States in a way they'd never seen his client before. Ironically, those convention ballroom gigs—which Tina was still committed to, even as the *Private Dancer* LP was about to be released—had served a purpose.

At least *that* portion of America was familiar with Tina. Now it was time to reintroduce Tina to America's large record-buying public. To do that, he needed to get Tina on the same bill as a superstar who drew a huge cross section of people.

In 1984, Lionel Richie's best-selling Motown album *Can't Slow Down* was battling Jackson's *Thriller* on the national music charts, selling millions of copies in the process. Here was a popular recording artist who was leading the charts, appealing to both blacks and whites, and who had a mature sound that would be perfectly complemented by Tina as an opening act. Richie's concerts attracted everyone from teenagers to grandparents. As it turned out, Richie himself, forever ahead of the crowd in the music game, was interested in Turner as his opening act. As Richie described it, when he went into the meeting with his manager Ken Kragen and other staffers, everyone pulled out a list of suggested opening acts for his tour. He wanted a *special* reaction. In that meeting, after everyone had emptied his own list, Richie said, "Well, I just have one name on my list—Tina Turner." Those in the room gasped in exhilaration.

Richie and Turner met on a soundstage in

Hollywood and began rehearsals. Tina recalled that she was immediately taken by Richie's singing voice. "In the studio, you can do a lot of things with the voice, but Lionel's was just as smooth live as it is on his records. That's a rarity."

The two got on instantly. They decided to do a couple of duets onstage together once the tour began and started rehearsing two songs—Richie's "Three Times a Lady" and the rambunctious "Hot Legs," made popular by rocker Rod Stewart. "Lionel said he wanted to do some rock and roll," said Tina. Today she still snickers when recalling the idea. "I said, 'Great!' We agreed on 'Hot Legs.' First we had to change the key. Then I asked him, 'Can we pick up the tempo?' He said, 'Sure, whatever you want.' So we started in on it again, and I asked to speed up the tempo just a little more. By then, it was really pumpin'. I think after the third day of rehearsal, Lionel had finally stopped sweating. It was hilarious—he was so out of breath."

By the time the Richie tour hit the road, *Private Dancer* was in the nation's record stores. The tour was the perfect combination—Richie's silky smooth ballads and Tina's driving rock and roll. The billing sold out concert venues across the country.

Onstage, the two exhibited a chemistry as natural as coffee and cream. One of the highlights of Richie's set was undoubtedly the moment when he'd call Tina to the stage for their burn-down-the-house version of "Hot Legs." Tina would playfully kick the musicians to the floor while they still played their instruments, as if her "hotness" caused them to collapse one by one, including Richie. One of the musicians reported that to spice up things some nights, when the microphone was away from her lips, Tina would whisper nasty nothings to each player. "She was a lot of fun. Every night. It wasn't like working for a living, that's for sure."

In the meantime, Davies' strategy was working. Aided by the rapid rise on the charts of the single "What's Love Got to Do with It," and bolstered by the Richie tour, the *Private Dancer* album was selling like hotcakes. Earlier, during the recording of the album, Tina had said that the album didn't have to sell millions of copies; she just wanted a hit record in both the States and Europe. Very soon, she would have all that she dreamed of and more. *Private Dancer* would go on to exceed the wildest dreams of everyone involved in the project.

8

The Queen Is Crowned

"God has blessed me with stamina and my health. I don't really do any incredible exercises. I guess what I do every night onstage has finally caught on."—Tina on her secret to her good looks.

Ottawa, Canada, was the place. Unlikely location for a rebirth, but for Tina it was as good a place as any. It was here, in yet another hotel ballroom, that Tina would play the last of all those gigs she lent her talents to in order to pay the debts left behind by her divorce from Ike. This gig was just like all the rest, except that it marked the very end of an era. Davies gracefully tried to pull Tina out of the commitment—she would be the main attraction at a gathering of McDonald's fast-food executives—but there was no way out. This crowd could care less that Tina Turner

149

had suddenly regained her status as a top rock star, and that the McDonald's date didn't live up to her new stature as a performer. Business was business. Besides, these guys, some of them downright rowdy after having tied one on, weren't looking to see someone like Wayne Newton. They wanted *Tina*.

Another of those ironic moments. While Tina sat in her nearby hotel room, *Private Dancer* was one of the hottest pieces of wax in the world. As she donned her wild wig, her single, the moody "What's Love Got to Do with It," was about to crack the number one position on the national charts. The record's success would free her from this kind of engagement, hopefully forever.

In the meantime, these men wanted a show, and that's what Tina set out to give them. As her band wound up the house with some driving rock and roll, out came Tina, prancing toward the mike stand to a groove that evolved into the distinctive sound of Prince's "Let's Pretend We're Married," the tune Tina frequently opened her shows with. It was a straight-ahead rock set, no more sequins, no more band members in oversized tuxedos. And at the end of this set, Tina turned the corner once and for all. Total payment on her future had finally been made.

And with a hit record and a successful United States tour with Lionel Richie under her belt, the future for Tina was movies. She'd been captured on celluloid before— Spector's *TNT Show,* which featured a lineup of hot sixties acts, also included the Ike and Tina Turner Revue. Then there was *Soul to Soul,* the film of the music festival, which featured Ike and Tina doing what they did best. And in 1975, director Ken Russell invited Tina to carry the role of the flamboyant Acid Queen in the rock musical *Tommy* an adaptation of a rock opera performed by the English band the Who. It wasn't a huge part; in fact, there were no spoken words. But it was enough to convince Tina that the big screen was something she really wanted to try her hand at. In addition to the role, she gained a true and lasting friend in Ann-Margret, the costar of the film, who encouraged her to pursue film roles seriously.

After she played a successful run of headline performances at Los Angeles' Beverly Theatre in 1984, Turner and Davies caught a flight to Australia, where they would rendezvous with director George Miller. He was extremely excited about the prospect of Tina appearing in one of his *Mad Max* movies. Miller had just about finished casting the third of these movies, *Mad Max Beyond Thunderdome*, but would leave the part of the sinister Auntie Entity open, just in case Tina decided to do it. Characteristically low-budget and heavy on the violence, the *Mad Max* films, with their barren futuristic settings, are in the same genre as Conan, but set in the year 2000. Still, the movies have won enough of an audience for an actor like the handsome Mel Gibson to launch a successful career from them.

According to Tina, however, her acting roles began long before *Tommy* or the role in *Mad Max* she ultimately nailed down. "As naughty as I appear to people," she told journalist Lisa Robinson, "it's an act. I'm an actress, and I've been working at it for years. That's as close as I come to explaining it. It's me out there onstage, but it's another me. I don't wear those rag dresses in everyday life—I'm always in pants. I'm not throwing my legs around all the time, either. If there's a guy out there who wants to bring that out in me," she laughed, "later on, when the lights are out, he's gonna have to set up a stage." Indeed, Tina is obviously a fine actress. For years, she pretended everything was good, when in fact those years were tough. "I had a job to do, and I did it well. The people come to see a show to get away from their own problems, not to listen to mine."

The idea of escapism appears to be paramount in Tina's entertainment plans. She has very little time for songwriting, but when asked what a Turner tune would sound like if she ever wrote one, she said, "It would be something very up; very optimistic. There's too much going on in the world right now that is negative. It would have to be something dealing in a positive manner."

Tina has said that her main concern in choosing acting roles is not to be typecast. "I've gotten plenty of offers, but I want to play someone away from my own person. Most of the roles offered to me have been that of a rock star or something. I want to do straight drama." Yet as this book goes to press, it was reported that Turner had turned down an offer from Quincy Jones to appear in his coproduction with Steven Spielberg of *The Color Purple,* a movie based on a somber megabestselling book of life in the South written by Alice Walker. "Let's face it, she's lived a lot of that kind of thing in her life," said one source. "Tina's ready to *live* a little. Her real life has been gray for a long time. She's ready for some bright spots." One who knows her film aspirations indicated that Tina is actually interested in doing more action films, like that of the *Mad Max* production. "Tina's a rocker at heart," he said. "She *really* is. I think the perfect combination for her would be to combine action with drama. That's where she's at right now."

Accordingly, reports from the *Mad Max* set suggested that Tina does indeed have a future in films. "She was a total professional," said a member of the crew in Australia, where most of the movie was shot. "She was on time, and she didn't freeze when the cameras started rolling. That's the most you can ask of anyone who doesn't make movies for a living. If they're on time at the set, then you can work with them. If they don't freeze up, you're bound to get *something* good down. But Tina had something to offer, so that's not her problem. I believe she'll end up like Cher. People laughed when she started making this big effort to be accepted as a serious actress. After she did *Silkwood* [starring Meryl Streep], they realized she could do it. Tina will make the change too."

Tina, who was reportedly paid a little more than $100,000 for her work in the *Mad Max* sequel emphasized the importance of having the opportunity to flex her muscles in the acting arena. "I've got to do this because it's something I've dreamed of. I can see myself doing some Broadway theater as well. I'm open to anything positive."

Increasingly, Tina has made it apparent that movies are something that she will pursue with a special enthusiasm. During interviews, she speaks more and more of her wishes to see herself on the silver screen. The last time she spoke so ardently of anything was when she began making it clear to the press of her interest in being recognized as a rock singer as opposed to an R & B singer. "When I used to work in the fields as a child," she said, "I daydreamed about being a movie star. I didn't think about the singing part too much, for I was already singing then—in the fields, at church, at talent shows, everywhere. I wanted to go past that. I wanted to be an actress. I still do."

Thus, films will play a major role in the progression of her career. She has indicated that ultimately, she'd like recordings and films to replace the touring. "My tours seem to last for years," she joked, "but I'd really enjoy doing a film every now and then and then making an album. I love doing it live, but as you know, the body can only take so much, and I've been out there for a while." If the quality of the roles offered Tina doesn't improve soon (although judging by *The Color Purple* offer, they appear to be getting better), it is easy to see how Tina and Davies, in the same fashion they resurrected her music career, may huddle and attempt to create their own cinematic vehicles, à la Barbra Streisand and Goldie Hawn. "I wouldn't rule that out one day," Tina has confessed. "Anything is possible."

Private Dancer had become one of the most positive professional things ever to happen to Tina. In March of 1985, Capitol Records took out a full-page color ad in *Billboard* magazine, a record-industry trade publication, to announce proudly that the album had sold more than three million copies worldwide. The album spawned four hit singles—"Let's Stay Together," "What's Love Got to Do with It," "Better Be Good to Me" and "Private Dancer"—and was getting tons of radio airplay nationally and was a favorite in clubs as well. It took two decades to do it, but finally Tina Turner was deemed a superstar.

Tina continued her foray into all the right places, making an appearance at the MTV Music Awards in New York, and, in cliché rock-star fashion, she put her now bankable vocals on the track "Tonight," by David Bowie. She was also in on the session for "I Want to Know What Love Is," the huge international hit for the band Foreigner—that's Tina wailing at the song's dramatic climax just before the fade-out.

However, even by the end of 1984, Tina's biggest moment was yet to come. Its prelude occurred January 28, 1985, at the American Music Awards, the annual pop ceremony presented by Dick Clark. There, Tina won the awards for Favorite Female Vocalist and Favorite Video Performer in the black music categories. (The night for her would end rather anticlimactically, when after being hailed by her musical peers as such a great performer, Tina performed "Private Dancer" by *lip-synching* to a recording.)

But Tina's crowning glory would come the very next month, during the biggie of all the pop music award shows, the Grammys. Perhaps an indication of spry musical times, the 1985 awards were literally up for grabs. Unlike 1984's show, when Michael Jackson's *Thriller* walked away with virtually every award except kudos in the gospel category, the 1985 competition was excitingly stiff. Lionel Richie, Bruce Springsteen, Cyndi

Lauper, and Prince and the Revolution were all acts that could conceivably steal the evening's thunder singlehandedly. In Los Angeles, backstage at the Shrine Auditorium, where the Awards were held, reporters and photographers were passing the time before the show wagering on the night's winners.

It wasn't easy for Tina. As her limousine drove her, Davies, her mother and the rest of her party into Los Angeles from her home in the affluent Los Angeles suburb of Sherman Oaks, she tried to contain her rabid emotions of excitement and fear. To win *anything* would bring Tina full circle, through hell and back. She had spent almost ten years picking up the pieces of her professional and personal life. To have a presenter open up any envelope and read her name would mean that beyond a hit record and all the surrounding hoopla, the music community actually recognized just where Tina had come from and where she was going.

As it turned out, Tina strode across the stage to that coveted podium three times— she was named Best Female Vocalist in both the pop and rock categories, while "What's Love Got to Do with It" won Best Record honors for songwriters Terry Britten and Graham Lyle. Not even the presence of

Prince, who also nabbed three Grammys and performed a rollicking version of "Baby, I'm a Star," could overshadow Tina's sparkling presence. The audience at the Shrine—luminaries like Kenny Rogers, Hall and Oates, Stevie Wonder and Cyndi Lauper—gave her standing ovations every time the superstar won an award.

Backstage, accompanied by her mother, Davies and others, Tina was the favorite of reporters and photographers, who virtually mobbed her for questions and shots. It seemed as if there was no one—even the people she was up against—who didn't want to see Tina go home with *something*. She cradled her awards for the flash pods and openly wept. "This is the greatest single moment in my career. . . . It was totally unexpected," she said. "When you win against the people I won against [Springsteen, Lauper], that's really winning."

Afterward, there were several parties— Capitol Records hosted one especially in her honor—but Tina couldn't mingle very long. Over at the A & M Records lot, a secret recording session was about to take place. The artists, a handful of America's finest, were assembling for the recording of "We Are the World," a single which would be sold to raise money to help the millions who are starving in Africa. The artists invited to participate read like a Who's Who of pop music. The prerequisites were a giving heart and, quite simply, superstardom. Tina Turner, with plenty of both, had no problem getting in that night.

Epilogue
A Star is Reborn

"I'd like to be remembered as an inspiration to young people. There are lots of little Michael Jacksons and others who have been inspired by their idols. I want there to be some little Tina Turners out there too."—Tina Turner, 1985.

If the atom bomb is ever dropped, Tina Turner just may absorb the blast and keep going. During her 45 years, she has probably encountered just about every emotion a person can experience, from acute pain to an almost euphoric bliss. "I feel like I've paid my debt to society, if there is such a thing," she has said, referring to her troubled past. "It's hard . . . it was hard for me . . . but I think it is possible for us as people to deal with more than we know. I believe we have the power to endure a lot. I've gone through a lot in my life, but I've managed to turn it around. All

161

of the times weren't great by any means, but I learned something from all of it."

Today Tina is proud of her life, who she is and what she has accomplished, especially raising a family under the circumstances they lived in during the years with Ike. Sons Craig, 26; Ronnie, 24; Ike Jr., 26; and Michael, 25, are all what she calls "straight ahead" men who are themselves musicians, having played behind their mother on occasion. "They're trying to get their thing together," Tina said, "but it can be difficult. Timing, the right songs, and on and on. I'm a living example."

Whether she realizes it or not, Tina Turner has become an entertainment institution. In the span of her career she has entertained three generations of fans. Her new success comes at a time when, and perhaps because, more than ever, pop music barriers are being crashed open. White audiences are embracing black artists, not to mention that black audiences are following white acts like David Bowie, Hall and Oates and Madonna. While Tina's comeback in Europe was phenomenal, in the States Michael Jackson, Lionel Richie and Prince opened doors for Tina Turner to have a comeback success as huge and across-the-board as *Private Dancer* turned out to be.

The fact that black recording artists now frequently top rock charts, added to her tremendous talent for making a song uniquely her own, makes Tina Turner one of the most popular entertainers in the world today. Considering the continued international sales of *Private Dancer,* Tina's concentrated move into the world of films, a 1985 HBO concert special, record-breaking concert tours, not to mention merchandising plans that include a clothing line among other spin-offs, it is easy to see how in 1985 Tina is becoming a mini-industry. She has also become a millionaire. Not surprisingly, with the fortune comes the fame—segments on the probing *20/20* television series, continued coverage in magazines like *Rolling Stone* and *People* and countless fanzines.

Another very important ingredient in Tina's smashing success was her appeal factor. In the music *business,* (as opposed to *creative* music endeavors—writing, producing and performing) some music executives, occupying plush office space far from the sound rooms where music is actually recorded, believe that a superstar only fills the gap left by a previous superstar. They believe that recording artists come in types. For example, Prince is said to fill the gap of superstars like Jimi Hendrix, Sly Stone and Little Richard. They believe that Prince could not have enjoyed such huge success had any of the aforementioned artists been thriving on the music scene. Prince can certainly be compared to those musicians, most of whom leaned toward a look of androgyny while specializing in a no-holds-barred brand of gutsy, emotional rock and roll. According to some of those who run their record company departments by this peculiar theory, Hall and Oates wouldn't have a chance if the blue-eyed soul duo the Righteous Brothers were still cranking out the hits. Likewise—though the statement could start a fight in some bars—Michael Jackson is filling the big-time G-rated rock throne left by Elvis.

If one uses that theory to measure Turner's chances of hitting the jackpot, then there is no way she could lose. First of all—and most importantly if you use the theory— there were no big female artists of Tina's stature on the scene when *Private Dancer* premiered in 1983. The existing pop princesses were holding court in their own categories. Diana Ross, both with the Supremes and as a solo artist, is one of the biggest female acts pop music has ever produced. But Ross wears diamond earrings and sings duets with Julio Iglesias; she's built a career on some of the great Top 40 songs over the years, and her chief exponent is glamour. She is the very best at what she does, but if artists were TV shows, Ross would be *Dynasty*—an image of money, luxurious townhouses and ritzy sophistication—and Turner would be *The "A" Team*—guts, excitement, a thrill a minute and action.

Donna Summer wasn't on the charts when Turner's *Private Dancer* was, but had she been, it would have been Ross who would have had to lose sleep since, according to the theory, Summer is deemed a hipper, younger model of Ross. As for the young female pop stars, namely Cyndi Lauper and Madonna, both of them hold distinctive posts. Lauper, whose image is that of a wacky but highly street-smart free spirit, is in her own stratosphere. Unquestionably, her music usually exhibits real emotionalism, maturity and coy realism. While all of these artists exploit their sexuality to some extent, sex is Madonna's chief exponent. Her trademark "Boy Toy" belt is what the glitter glove is to Michael Jackson, what a purple trench coat is to Prince. The idea is a singing personification of a sexy blonde like Marilyn Monroe. Madonna is the girl who lived on every boy's block, stayed out late at night and knew more about sex than anyone else. It's an act that has made Madonna a media item, this year's Cabbage Patch™ doll.

Tina Turner is something else altogether. Naturally funkier than Ross, possessing more raw energy onstage than Lauper, and making the Madonna idea of sexuality look like, well, child's play. Tina is a woman who rose from one-nighters on the "chitlin' circuit" to almost having it all, who lost it all, only to get back what she had lost and then some. Some experiences are like a badge— they tend to show. There was not another top female singer who could compete with her at the time of Tina's reemergence. According to the theory, there was no way she could lose.

For Tina, the age factor was also important. Though recent research has since refuted the idea, those same music-business types who hold tight to this theory also believe that the bulk of pop records today are purchased by an age group that generally falls between ten and twenty-five. New evidence, including the recognition of "yuppies," that demographic of sixties kids who've grown up to be upwardly mobile, credit-card–carrying achievers, now suggests that there is an even wider age range of hard-core pop record buyers that reaches way beyond thirty. Today's pop star aspires to tap that reservoir of youth in the same way artists like Jackson, Prince and Richie have been able to attract all races of the record-buying public. "You can feel the difference when an artist is selling records to everybody," said one Capitol Records official. "Look at Bruce Springsteen. He's a quality act, yet he reaches only half the audience, say, a Michael Jackson or a Prince does. Those artists double and even triple what he sells because everyone is buying their records—black, white, and of course, in Prince's case, purple."

Tina, having had a very successful first career whose following was primarily an adult audience, was certainly aware of the high stakes involved in selling platters to *everyone* when *Private Dancer* was released in 1983. "I want everyone to know who Tina Turner is," she told a press conference about the time of the LP's release. "This is a new day; music appeals to everyone—why shouldn't it?"

For all her reborn celebrity status, Tina

leads a relatively quiet life. She keeps a pulse on her business matters and, by show-business standards, is extremely discreet. Despite her newfound wealth, her indulgences have been few. Recently, she purchased a Mercedes Jeep in Europe and had it shipped to her Sherman Oaks home, but otherwise she simply enjoys life. "I'm a basic person," she has insisted. "I like nice things, but I don't go too far out." As far as the new fame is concerned, "I like it. I can't deny that. But I prefer to keep both feet on the ground. Now that I've reached a certain level, I can see how people can't handle this and go crazy. You've got people telling you all these wonderful things and they want to do everything for you. That's great—I can enjoy it. But I know what's what. I won't be walking on water anytime soon." Indeed. There are days that Zelma, Tina's mother, probably feels the crunch of fame more than her daughter. A manicurist in a Beverly Hills salon, she has become a bit of a celebrity herself. Tina has fought hard to protect the privacy of those around her, especially the current love interest in her life. She has confided that there have been "younger men," but goes no further. The Hollywood rumor mill has linked her with, among others, record producer

Richard Perry, the force behind the success of the Pointer Sisters. For Tina, however, mum's the word.

Almost as captivating as Tina's remarkable musical talent is her amazing ability to maintain her youthful beauty. However, those looking to the entertainer for any special beauty secrets will probably be surprised to learn that there *are* none. "I just think that I'm fortunate in this lifetime to be youthful at my age and maintain my appearance," she has said. "I'm not one of those people who gets in a jogging suit and comes running out of the house, huffing along. When I'm off the road, I'm usually just lounging around the house. I love being there when I can. But it just so happens that my work keeps me in shape."

For the most part, Tina, while delivering songs like "Proud Mary" and "Be Good to Me," gets as much or more exercise than the average woman clad in designer tights and struggling to keep up with Jane Fonda's exercise record. Anyone who has seen Turner perform knows the regimen—dancing, strutting, sweating under the lights, working those lungs, developing her coordination. It's a grinding routine that goes on for an hour and a half, night after night. It doesn't help that Tina is often at the mercy of food on the road—lousy hotel cuisine, plastic airplane gourmet and restaurants in small towns where the menus aren't as elaborate as those in major cities.

Still, just good old-fashioned basic body maintenance is Tina's only tool. "I'm lucky in the fact that I keep in shape and get paid for it," she laughed. Tina has admitted that as a child she didn't particularly care for her looks. "I didn't like myself very much because I was very thin when I was growing up," she once told a reporter. "I had what we called a high fanny, long legs, high cheekbones and a big mouth. It all just wasn't very stylish back then, especially in Tennessee."

Oddly enough, it's her legs that Tina says she hated the most in those early days. "It's strange how my legs are to me; sometimes they look pretty and sometimes they don't," she said. "I am fortunate that my feet look pretty good in shoes, and that makes my legs look nice." Remarkably, Tina's legs look better today than they did in her more youthful days of the Revue. "I'm older; I'm settled," she remarked. "It's all gotten into place."

Tina insists that she's never had to diet. "I've spent most of my life losing five pounds a night," she said, though she does watch what she consumes. "I used to eat a lot of pork, fried foods and bread. I just love bread with lots of butter. But, I've learned moderation. I really do think that's it for anything. It won't matter how long you work out at the gym if you're doing the same unhealthy things when you come out of there."

In 1984, Tina was asked how long she would continue to perform, "I'll stop when my body says it's time to stop. I still have fun up there on the stage. Sometimes I forget how old I am, honestly. Age is only a number, especially if you can stay healthy and beautiful and take on the wisdom you get from the numbers."

If Roger Davies is to be remembered as the man who helped bring Tina Turner's career out of the doldrums, then it is the star herself who must be credited with engineering what can only be called the Tina Turner look. It is a look that is a contradiction in many ways: the outrageous coupled with the original, used together to create a look that is distinctively Tina. "I never wanted to do what people told me I should," she's said. "Everyone felt I should dress my age. Well, I've never felt my age, so I didn't know what they meant by that. I guess they meant a more 'mature' look. But I've always felt comfortable doing my own thing."

According to Tina, the way she looked in the sixties, was almost totally Ike's vision. "The way I looked back then was his creation," she said. "By looking at me today, you can see the differences in what I wanted and what he wanted." Today, Tina prefers her hair styled in an "eighties wild." (She once told a writer that she hadn't been in the public without a wig in years.) She now wears a minimum of makeup. At the 1985 American Music Awards, Tina was the personification of her mesh of fashion. A dark, two-piece suit boasting short pants to show off her trademark legs, in sexy black fishnet stockings to offset the suit's almost classic cut. On her lapel she wore a trendy rhinestone military medal that worked with her dazzling earrings. The ensemble was classy, yet distinctively rock and roll.

But Tina has also had to endure her share of criticism about her rock and roll image. Some critics point out that the singer has been too resounding in what they call her campaign to disassociate herself from R & B music. "It hurts," said one journalist, "to see that she finds it necessary to down R & B all the time, when that's what she is—an R & B singer. There's nothing wrong with that and someone should tell her. In interviews, she's always mentioning the fact that she's always been a rock and roll singer. Rock and roll *is* black music. An R & B song [Al Green's "Let's Stay Together"] is what fueled her comeback. Tina's from the same blues school as Etta James and Aretha Franklin; she should be proud of that." Tina also received flak from various humanitarian and civil rights groups, the National Association for the Advancement of Colored People (NAACP) included, for a performance she did in apartheid-ridden South Africa during her hungry years. Tina's management subsequently presented a formal apology to the organizations involved, and Tina's career has suffered no ill affects from the disclosure.

As for Ike, in recent years he has kept an extremely low profile. His dealings in entertainment, at least publicly, have come to a complete halt. In 1983, however, Ike was stopped in Los Angeles for a minor traffic violation; while searching his vehicle, police officers found a substance they thought to be cocaine. Ike was held, all the while insisting that what he was carrying was anything but cocaine. Police conducted tests on the white powder. Several days later, they issued a statement, a rather embarrassing admission, that what they found in Ike Turner's car was not an illegal substance.

Since then the musician's whereabouts have been hard to pinpoint. This writer did happen to see Ike in a local Los Angeles restaurant, dining with Charlie Wilson, lead singer for an R & B group called the Gap Band. But other reports suggested that after Ike's arrest he migrated for a brief while to St. Louis. Recently there has been talk on the Hollywood musicians' circuit that Ike, well aware of the newfound interest in the Ike and Tina legend, was planning to hold auditions for black and white Ikettes, in hopes of putting together an eighties-style Revue.

The most concrete evidence that Ike has a definite interest in staging his own comeback comes from Alan Mink, who manages Teena Marie, a Columbia recording artist who recently enjoyed the success of a Top 10 pop/R & B hit, "Lover Girl." According to Mink, Ike phoned one day with the sincere offer that Marie and he do a national concert tour together, thus allowing Ike to bill the shows as "The Ike and Teena Show." "He was very polite," said Mink, "and it sounded like he was calling from right here in Los Angeles. I told him that I would introduce the idea to

my client and get back to him." Nothing ever
came of the situation and, as of this writing,
Ike remains in artistic oblivion.

After years of being up at bat, Tina has
finally attained the brilliant success that she
dreamed of years ago as a child back in Nutbush, Tennessee. Yet, for all of the material
glory, Tina sees a distant future quite unlike
that of most entertainers. Certainly million-
selling records, movie roles and maybe even
Broadway are goals. But for Tina there is still
another goal. She has said that she'll perform
until she's about fifty and then devote her life
to spreading the word of Buddha.

According to Turner, if she is ever as
closely associated with Buddhism as other
entertainers have been linked with their beliefs and causes, she will welcome the association. Over and over in interviews, she has
credited Buddhism as the lone force that
pulled her up from the emotional trenches in
which she found herself after her stormy
marriage. today, Tina keeps a small altar in
her home. Every morning that she is at
home, she kneels before it and begins her
chant, which, repeated over and over swiftly,
sounds not like words, but a droning hum.
She continues the ritual when on the road. "I
would call it a recharger," she has said. "To

sit on the floor and chant just before a show or even an important meeting can give you confidence. The confidence comes from the feeling. You've plugged into a special energy. You can make it work for you."

For all the earthy grit she exhibits onstage and in her songs, Tina's spiritual beliefs are lofty but firm. She is an avowed believer in reincarnation. "Oh, definitely," she told *Ebony* magazine three years ago. "I really believe that I've been on this earth before. I think all the situations that occur when something seems a little more familiar than usual—those things are more than coincidences."

"That's what I want to do," she insisted. "I believe that is why I'm here, why I've gone through such a rough time—to have the experience to talk about. If I was just a nobody, people would not listen. But after I really get their attention, I'd like to share something with them." It is an unlikely path for a world-famous superstar, but at this point, one is led to believe that if anything can be done, then Tina Turner can do it.

The stunning success of *Private Dancer* exceeded Tina's wildest dreams. Now she looks forward to more hit records and the prospect of becoming a bona fide movie star. *Photo courtesy of Capitol Records.*

Discography

To compile a *total* listing of Ike and Tina Turner recordings is something I doubt even Tina herself could do. As mentioned in the text, in the early days Ike Turner made deals with labels at the drop of a hat—often just one-shot deals that would only cover an album or a single. Thanks to the Michael Ochs Archives, the following list is probably as comprehensive as one can get, considering the fact that most of the companies that released them are no longer in business, and that those which are still around aren't press-

179

ing these records anymore. You'll notice the absence of release dates. That's because many of the originals simply did not include the information. Those records that do have dates are reissues of original material from the fifties and sixties. If you've got any of the originals in your possession, hang onto them. Tina Turner's superstar status has made them collector's items.

ALBUMS

Ike Turner and his Kings of Rhythm,
Volume One,
Ace/Cadet 5669

The Legendary Ike Turner and
the Kings of Rhythm,
Hey Hey,
Red Lightnin' RL 0047

Ike Turner's Kings of Rhythm,
I'm Tore Up,
Red Lightnin' RL 0016

Ike Turner's Kings of Rhythm and
Harold Burrage,
Rockin' Wild!
P-Vine Special PLP-9021

Ike Turner,
Rocks the Blues,
Crown 5367

Ike Turner,
Blues Roots,
United Artists 5576

Ike and Tina Turner,
It's Gonna Work Out Fine,
Sue 2007

Ike and Tina Turner,
The Soul of Ike and Tina Turner,
Sue 2001

Ike and Tina Turner,
Don't Play Me Cheap,
Sue SLP 2005

Ike and Tina Turner's Kings of Rhythm,
Dance,
Sue 2003

Ike and Tina Turner,
Dynamite,
Sue 2004

Ike and Tina Turner,
The Greatest Hits of Ike and Tina Turner,
Sue 1038

Ike and Tina Turner,
Hot 'n' Sassy,
Accord SN 7147

Ike and Tina Turner,
So Fine,
Pompeii SD 6000

Ike and Tina Turner,
Get It—Get It,
Cenco 104

Ike and Tina Turner,
Get It Together,
Pompeii SD 6006

Ike and Tina Turner Revue,
Live,
Kent KST 514

Ike and Tina Turner and the Ikettes,
In Person,
Mint LP 2408

Ike and Tina Turner Show,
Live,
Warner Brothers WS 1579

Ike and Tina Turner Show,
Volume II,
Loma 5904

Ike and Tina Turner,
16 Great Performances,
ABC ABTD-4014

Ike and Tina Turner,
The Hunter,
Blue Thumb BTS11

Ike and Tina Turner,
River Deep—Mountain High,
London SHU 8298

The Raelets with Ike and Tina Turner,
Souled Out,
Tangerine TRCS-1511

Ike and Tina Turner and the Ikettes,
Come Together,
Liberty LST-7637

Ike and Tina,
What You Hear Is What You Get,
United Artists UAS-9953

Ike and Tina Turner,
Live in Paris,
Liberty LBS 834689

Ike and Tina Turner,
Let Me Touch Your Mind,
United Artists UA-5660 0598

Ike and Tina Turner,
Working Together,
Liberty LST-7650

Ike and Tina Turner,
Her Man . . . His Woman,
Capitol ST-571

Ike and Tina Turner,
'Nuff Said,
United Artists UAS-5530

Ike and Tina Turner,
Feel Good,
United Artists UA5598

Ike and Tina Turner,
Nutbush City Limits,
United Artists LA 180-F

Ike and Tina Turner,
The Gospel According to Ike and Tina,
United Artists UA-44678

Ike and Tina Turner,
The World of Ike and Tina,
United Artists UA-LA064-G2 6698

184

Ike and Tina Turner,
The Best of Ike and Tina Turner,
Blue Thumb BTS49

Ike and Tina Turner,
Greatest Hits,
United Artists UA-LA592-G

Tina Turner,
Rough,
United Artists UA-LA919-14

Tina Turner,
Private Dancer,
Capitol, ST-12330

SINGLES

Ike Turner and his Kings of Rhythm,
"Do You Mean It"/"She Made My Blood
Run Cold,"
Federal 12297

Ike and Tina Turner,
"I Made a Promise Up Above"/

"Dear John,"
Sue 146

Ike and Tina Turner,
"A Fool in Love,"/
"The Way You Love Me,"
Sue 730

Ike and Tina Turner,
"I Idolize You"/
"Letter from Tina,"
Sue 735

Ike and Tina Turner,
"You're My Baby"/"I'm Jealous,"
Sue 740

Ike and Tina Turner,
"It's Gonna Work Out Fine"/"Won't You
Forgive Me,"
Sue 749

Ike and Tina Turner,
"Poor Fool"/"You Can't Blame Me,"
Sue

Ike and Tina Turner,
"Tra La La La La"/"You Can't Blame Me,"
Sue

Ike and Tina Turner,
"You Should'a Treated Me
Right"/"Sleepless,"
Sue 765

Ike and Tina Turner,
"So Fine"/"So Blue Over You,"
Innis 666

Ike and Tina Turner,
"Hurt Is All You Gave"/"Goodbye,
So Long,"
Modern MM 1007-1

Ike and Tina Turner,
"He's the One,"/"Chicken Shack,"
Kent K 418-1

Ike and Tina Turner,
"Please, Please Please"
(Pts. 1&2) Kent K4514

Ike and Tina Turner,
"Dust My Broom,"/"I'm Hooked,"
Tangerine TRC-269-266

Ike and Tina Turner,
"You Can't Miss Nothing That You Never
Had" (both sides),
Sonja 2005

Ike and Tina Turner,
"You Weren't Ready"/"Get It–Get it,"
Cenco 112-A

Ike and Tina Turner,
"River Deep–Mountain High,"/"I'll Keep
You Happy,"
Philles 131

Ike and Tina Turner,
"I'll Never Need More than This"/"The
Cashbox Blues,"
Philles 135

Ike and Tina Turner,
"A Man Is a Man Is a Man"/"Two To
Tango"
Philles 134

Ike and Tina Turner,
"I've Been Loving You Too Long"/"Crazy
'bout You Baby,"
Blue Thumb BTA 202

Ike and Tina Turner
"The Hunter"
Blue Thumb BLU 102

Ike and Tina Turner,
"Tell Her I'm Not Home"/"I'm Thru with
Love,"
Loma 2011

Ike and Tina Turner,
"A Fool for a Fool"/"No Tears to Cry,"
Warner Brothers 5433

Ike and Tina Turner and the Ikettes,
"I Want to Take You Higher"/"Contact
High,"
Liberty 56177

JULIO!

BY JEFF ROVIN

'I need a woman more than life itself'

Julio Iglesias. He breaks records – and hearts – in performances around the world. And the qualities that make his songs so exciting – sensuality, vulnerability, raw emotion – are the same qualities that he brings to every aspect of his private life.

In this book, you will learn all about Julio Iglesias, the man. About the crippling automobile accident that ended his dreams of becoming a professional soccer player and ultimately launched him into his new career as a singer. About his many torrid romances, including his love affair with Priscilla Presley. About his close and loving relationship with his father and his inspiring relationship with his daughter. About his goals for the future, both on and off the stage.

As memorable as an Iglesias performance.

As intimate as an Iglesias song.

0 553 17200 X   £1.95

DON'T FALL OFF THE MOUNTAIN

by Shirley MacLaine

'I've always felt that I would never develop into a really fine actress because I cared more about life beyond the camera than the life in front of it. Over the years my search became broader and broader. After two months on a picture my car seemed to veer toward the airport of its own accord. I still loved acting and enjoyed it. I was a professional, but basically I was more interested in the people I played than the movies I played them in . . .'
Shirley MacLaine

An outspoken thinker, a keen observer, a truly independent woman, Shirley MacLaine takes us on a remarkable journey into her life and her inner self. From her Virginia roots, to stardom, marriage, motherhood and her enlightening travels to mysterious corners of the world, her story is exciting and poetic, moving and humorous – the varied and life-changing experiences of a talented, intelligent and extraordinary woman.

0 553 23662 8   £2.50